INTUITION

Its Nature and Uses
in Human Experience

INTUITION
Its Nature and Uses in Human Experience

HOPE K. FITZ, Ph. D.

MOTILAL BANARSIDASS PUBLISHERS
PRIVATE LIMITED ● DELHI

First Edition: Delhi, 2001
Reprint: Delhi, 2002

© MOTILAL BANARSIDASS PUBLISHERS PRIVATE LIMITED
All Rights Reserved.

ISBN: 81-208-1772-9

Also available at:

MOTILAL BANARSIDASS

41 U.A. Bungalow Road, Jawahar Nagar, Delhi 110 007
8 Mahalaxmi Chamber, 22 Bhulabhai Desai Road, Mumbai 400 026
120 Royapettah High Road, Mylapore, Chennai 600 004
236, 9th Main III Block, Jayanagar, Bangalore 560 011
Sanas Plaza, 1302 Baji Rao Road, Pune 411 002
8 Camac Street, Kolkata 700 017
Ashok Rajpath, Patna 800 004
Chowk, Varanasi 221 001

Printed in India
BY JAINENDRA PRAKASH JAIN AT SHRI JAINENDRA PRESS,
A-45 NARAINA, PHASE-I, NEW DELHI 110 028
AND PUBLISHED BY NARENDRA PRAKASH JAIN FOR
MOTILAL BANARSIDASS PUBLISHERS PRIVATE LIMITED,
BUNGALOW ROAD, DELHI 110 007

This book is dedicated to:
my dear departed friend
Margaret Dell Jewett, Ph.D.
(1924 - 1998)

TABLE OF CONTENTS

PREFACE

In this book, I explore the nature and uses of intuition in human experience. The overall position which I present is that intuition is a natural and necessary part of the "mind's life," i.e., the functioning of the human mind in the process of acquiring knowledge. Furthermore, without an appeal to intuition, much of human experience is either inadequately explained or inexplicable. Hence, the nature and uses of intuition need to be understood, and, as with intelligence, intuition needs to be developed.

A major challenge which I have had to address in undertaking the subject of intuition is that many philosophers and thinkers either ignore or reject intuition. As I shall explain in Chapter I, the epistemological thrust, which started in what is called the "modern period" of Western philosophy (from the time of Descartes, 1596–1650, until roughly the end of the 19th century) and persists into what is usually referred to as the "recent period" (from the end of the modern period until the present), has continued to grow in importance, and has greatly influenced the views about knowledge and the rigor required in the reasoning process. Given this epistemological thrust, intuition, as it has been described, is simply not acceptable to rigorous thinkers. As we shall see, the Western traditional view of intuition, as well as the ancient non-Western traditional view of intuition held by the Hindus, has been, and continues to be, that it is a nondiscursive form or an independent way of gaining knowledge. Yet, as most rigorous thinkers hold, knowledge is taken to be discursive by its very nature. This means that if I make a claim to knowledge, I must be able to offer and substantiate reasons for the claim in order to justify it.

Early in my research on the subject of intuition, I found in the writings of Sarvepalli Radhakrishnan, a Hindu philosopher, a core idea as to what intuition is. This idea enabled me to develop a view as to the nature of intuition which is not at odds with what rigorous thinkers take knowledge to be, namely, a discursive process of the mind, or the result thereof. According to my account, intuition is **not** a nondiscursive form or independent way of gaining knowledge. However, it is, I argue, **one means** to knowledge, which is complementary to and can be checked by reason. I have identified two kinds of intuition, namely, penetrative and creative, which I shall explain in Chapter II.

Another major challenge, and actually a stumbling block, in writing this book was the subject matter in Chapter V, namely, the use of intuition in what is sometimes referred to as the "spiritual experience" or "mystical experience." I call this an area of "transcendent awareness" or simply "transcendence". As I shall explain in Chapter V, it is intuition and revelation which form transcendent awareness. This view of transcendence is novel, and I believe that it is important, because without it, I see no way to speak meaningfully about any ultimate reality. After all, every sacred book is based on either an insight into and/or a revelation concerning reality.

I had difficulty gaining a direction for the aforementioned chapter, until I was invited to present a paper on the subject of transcendence at the Karl Jaspers Society of North America. In the paper, "The Role of Intuition and Revelation in Transcendence," I was able to combine my work on intuition, specifically penetrative insight, with Martin Heidegger's account of Revealed Being, so that I could offer some view as to how humans can gain an awareness of, and perhaps even some understanding of, what is revealed in transcendence.

In addition to the foregoing themes, I offer an account of justification of a belief, and argue that since intuition is one means to knowledge, certain beliefs can be justified by an appeal to intuition, thereby expanding the criteria for claims to knowledge. Also, I offer a definition and account of creativity which reflect aspects of both the traditional view that creativity is a gift of genius, i.e., one is either born with it or not, and the contemporary view that all persons have a potential for creativity, but some persons develop it, and some do not. According to my view, creativity is an ability, and all persons are born with a potential for creativity. However, the potential differs from person to person.

Two people whom I wish to thank for their support, encouragement and insights are: Stephen A. Erickson, E. Wilson Lyon Professor of Humanities, and Professor of Philosophy, at Pomona College, and the late Dr. Margaret Dell Jewett, Assistant Professor of Philosophy, retired from California State University, Los Angeles. I also wish to thank John Hutchison, Professor of Philosophy, Emeritus, from Claremont Graduate School, for his input into my early studies of intuition, and his help in establishing a Comparative Philosophy Degree program for me. It was within this degree program that I was able to undertake my early work on intuition.

In addition to those persons whom I have mentioned, I want to express my gratitude to: Dr. Sarah Langley, Associate Professor of Anthropology, Emeritus, from Eastern Connecticut State University, who edited the manuscript; Mr. Madhu Reddy, Academic Computing Support Specialist at Eastern Connecticut State University, who both formatted the document and helped to decode the program for the diacritical marks, and Mrs. Annette Bradstreet, Secretary for Sociology, the Social Work Program and Canadian Studies Program at Eastern Connecticut State University. Mrs. Bradstreet helped with the typing decoding and entering the diacritical marks, as well as the final editing of those marks.

Finally, I wish to thank Dr. David Carter, President of Eastern Connecticut State University, and my colleagues at ECSU. These people had confidence in my ability to complete this project.

INTRODUCTION

From ancient times until the present, intuition is mentioned, discussed, or implied in both Western and non-Western philosophical writings.[1] In general, I take Western philosophy to include: the philosophical quest and the philosophies which began in ancient Greece,[2] those philosophies which had their origins in Greek philosophy, and the philosophies which were influenced not only by the Greek philosophical heritage, but, also by the Judeo/Christian religious tradition.[3] Even though intuition has been considered in the foregoing writings, accounts as to the nature of intuition, and how it functions, are not common. Nevertheless, there is what I take to be a traditional Western philosophical view of what intuition is. As I shall explain, this view, although influenced by ancient Western philosophical thought, seems to have taken form in the medieval thinking of the scholastics. In addition to the traditional Western philosophical view as to the nature of intuition, there is a traditional Hindu philosophical view of what intuition is which appears to predate the Western view by hundreds of years.[4]

Traditionally, in both the Western and non-Western Hindu philosophical schools of thought, which I will discuss in Chapter I, intuition has been taken to be a non-discursive form or independent way of gaining knowledge. The problem with accepting these traditional views of intuition is that they "fly in the face" of what rigorous thinkers take knowledge to be, namely, a discursive process and/or the result thereof.

Given the traditional view as to the nature of intuition, many modern and contemporary philosophers, and rigorous thinkers in general, have either rejected or ignored any consideration of it. However, as I shall make clear, intuition is a natural part of the "mind's life," or human life, without which much of what humans experience or claim to know is either understandable only according to some reductionist theory of explanation (a theory which reduces experience to an explanation of a particular discipline, e.g., a psychological, cultural, or biological explanation, etc.), or simply inexplicable. Examples of human experiences involving intuition that are often analyzed according to some reductionist theory which ignores intuition are: (1) "a calling" to a particular vocation or field of endeavor; (2) certain scientific discoveries; (3) acts or works of creativity; (4) insights concerning the resolution of problems and difficult situations, e.g., whether to take a new position or job which would enable one to develop certain desired talents, or skills, or to remain in a position which offers more security; (5) an entrepreneur's ability to foresee eventualities regarding future profits that others do not see; and (6) insights into one's own process of development or self-realization.

Included in the beliefs which are. ultimately inexplicable without an appeal to intuition, and/or revelation, are both: (1) traditional metaphysical beliefs concerning the nature of ultimate reality or reality entire, and/or (2) beliefs in a transcendent or an ultimate Being or "Ultimate," which are not based simply on faith and/or acceptance of a particular dogma.

Considering what I have said above, one is faced with a dilemma. On the one hand, intuition is a natural and necessary part of the "mind's life;" which is needed in order to explain much of human experience, and, on the other hand, the traditional views as to the nature of intuition are not acceptable to rigorous thinkers.

After years of comparative (Western/non-Western) research on the subject of intuition,[5] I have undertaken the task of explaining the nature of intuition in such a way as to legitimate it so that it will be acceptable to even the most rigorous of thinkers.

In addition to explaining the nature of intuition, I also describe its uses in: (1) everyday life; (2) creativity; and (3) transcendent awareness which some philosophers and theologians have called the "mystical experience," or the "spiritual experience."

In order to understand what intuition is, and how it functions, it must, where possible, be considered apart from any presuppositions as to the nature of an "Ultimate." As I shall make clear in the book, such presuppositions have shaped traditional views about intuition. However, I argue that an understanding of the nature of intuition cannot be determined by a particular ontological view. In fact, to the contrary, as I shall explain, it is the intuition of what is revealed (in the Heideggerian sense of *es gibt*, i.e., what is given in experience) that enables humans to have an understanding of those aspects of mundane existence which cannot be known by sense experience alone. Also, as I shall explain in the last chapter of the book, one kind of intuition, namely penetrative insight, together with revelation, in the Heideggerian sense, accounts for transcendent awareness.

By way of procedure, in the first chapter, I reiterate that although there are many references to intuition both in Western and non-Western philosophy, there are few accounts as to its nature and function. However, as I mentioned earlier, and emphasize again, there are two traditional views of the subject: one Western, and the other a non-Western Hindu view. First, I will explore and criticise the traditional Western view. Then I will explore and criticise a Western non-traditional view of intuition found in the philosophy of Henri Bergson. Finally, I will explore the traditional Hindu view of intuition. In the critique of each of the foregoing views, I will argue that intuition cannot be a non-discursive form or independent way of gaining knowledge.

In the second chapter of the book, I will explain what I take intuition to be. In so doing, I give credit to Sarvepalli Radhakrishnan for the core idea of the subject which I culled from his writings. However, as I shall make clear, my view of intuition differs markedly from his, as his view presupposes a Hindu notion of ultimate reality, and knowledge of that reality. Furthermore, he accepts the traditional Hindu view that intuition is a higher form of knowledge than what is gained by reason. My view, as I indicated earlier, rests on no such presupposition, and I argue that intuition is not a non-discursive form or independent way of gaining knowledge, but only one means to knowledge. After, explaining what I take intuition to be, I will make clear two different kinds of intuition which I have identified, namely, penetrative insight, and creative insight. Then I will describe the uses of both of these kinds of intuition in everyday life, including the use of intuition in making decisions concerning business, health, relationships, etc. Finally, I shall explain that a successful use of intuition has to be developed.

In the third chapter of the book, I will consider certain philosophies which reject or ignore intuition as a means to knowledge, and argue that such views limit human understanding and knowledge unnecessarily. Later I will briefly consider various beliefs which involve an appeal to intuition for justification. I will argue that these beliefs meet the logical requirements for a warranted conclusion in an informal inductive argument. Finally, I conclude that since intuition is one means to knowledge, as I argued in chapter II, and have shown in the aforementioned arguments, it should be recognized as one criterion for the justification of a belief.

The fourth chapter of the book is devoted to the use of intuition in creativity. After much research,[6] and teaching courses on the subject,[7] I define creativity as: the ability to visualize, or foresee, and generate ideas, or the expressions or creations thereof, which are original — ranging from imaginative to inventive, and from inventive to ingenious; and of effect and/or value. My explanation of the nature of creativity embraces aspects of both the traditional view that creativity is a gift, and the contemporary belief that all persons have a potential for creativity. According to my explanation, the potential for creativity differs from person to person. Hence, the development of the various potentials results in differing degrees of creativity, ranging from simple acts of imagination, e.g., choosing one's wardrobe, to the acts of genius. In general, the term "genius" has been conferred upon a person when what she/he produces is judged to be original in the sense of radically different, and of far reaching effect and great value. In this chapter, I appeal to two renowned scholars, who have written about the use of intuition in creativity, in order to substantiate my view that intuition is a necessary component of creativity. To be specific, I appeal to the writings of Jules Henri Poincaré, the great mathematician of the last century, and Michael Polanyi, the renowned scientist and philosopher of the early part of this century.

In the fifth chapter of the book, I put forth the view that a particular kind of intuition, namely, penetrative insight, together with revelation (in the Heideggerian sense) together form transcendence. As I shall explain, it is penetrative insight at a very developed level, which makes possible transcendent awareness. Also, although there is a range of transcendent awareness, it is the higher level of that range which some philosophers and theologians have referred to as the "spiritual experience" or "mystical experience," with which I am concerned.

Finally, I want to make clear why I do not take up the use of intuition by those engaged in areas of psychic phenomena. The reason is that those purported to be psychic (and I am convinced that some persons have psychic abilities)[8] hold various metaphysical views as to the nature of reality. In order to study this psychic phenomena thoroughly, someone would have to examine the psychic insights, which are obviously intuitive, and, as far as possible, intellectually separate those insights from the different metaphysical presuppositions. Also, the insights must be separated from certain superstitions and actions relating to magic. I am very wary of beliefs in magic, as magic has to do with the desire and/ or need to control one's environment. This desire is linked to a person's sense of ego, and as the great Hindu philosopher, Patañjali, who wrote the *Yoga Sūtra*, over two thousand years ago,[9] recognized, supra-normal insight, or what I call "transcendent awareness," can be lost if one stays attached to ego, or ego-centric desires.[10]

Because it is so difficult to separate superstition and magic from psychic phenomena, and my areas of expertise and interest fall more within the realm of metaphysics and epistemology, I will leave the writing on the use of intuition in psychic phenomena to some other scholar.

ENDNOTES

1. In Western philosophy, we find intuition mentioned or discussed
    from the ancient period of Greek philosophy, e.g., Plato in the
    "Phaedo," to the recent or present period. However, it is the
    medieval period that I take to be the source of the traditional
    Western view of intuition. (I will discuss this view in depth in
    Chapter I.)

    In Hindu philosophy, the sacred text of the Hindus, i.e., the
    Vedas, is based upon darśana or insight. It is believed that via this
    insight the seers (ṛṣi means seer) were able to see into reality. In
    fact, the Hindu schools of philosophy who accept the authority of
    the *Vedas* are called *darśanas*. In Hindu philosophical thought,
    darśana is a means to knowledge, central to a method of self-
    realization, i.e., jñāna yoga, and a higher form of knowledge. We
    find many writings on insight or intuition by Hindu philosophers
    and thinkers, but the views put forth are based on, or reflect, the
    traditional view of Patañjali in the ancient *Yoga Sūtra* which he
    wrote. (I discuss Patañjali's view in Chapters I and V.)

2. I do not mean to imply that there were not non-Greek influences
    on early Greek philosophical thought. In fact, I, as many compara-
    tive philosophers, am impressed by the obvious Hindu influence
    on much of early Greek thinking (Socrates, Plato, Plotinus, etc.)

3. Most of Western philosophy seems to be traceable to this Greek-
    Judeo/Christian influence. Even the philosophical systems or move-
    ments which seem removed from this line of thinking, are, in
    general, the result of reactions against it.

4. In the text A *Sourcebook in Indian Philosophy*, p. 453, the editors,
    Sarvepalli Radhakrishnan and Charles A. Moore, place the time of
    Patañjali, i.e., the author of the Yoga school, as the second century
    B.C.

5. I started work on my doctoral dissertation in 1978. I have continued
    to do research relating to intuition. Five papers, relating to intu-
    ition, have been published in scholarly journals, and I have
    presented numerous papers at conferences on the subject. Also,
    I have been working on this book for about ten years, off and on.

6. In 1987, I spent the entire year, as a reader at the Huntington
    Research Library in San Marino, California, working on the subject.

7. In 1986, at Mount St. Mary's College, Los Angeles, I was privileged
    to work with Dr. Elizabeth Sewell, the renowned Newton and
    William Blake scholar (who is recognized as a poet in her own right)
    on the subject of "Genius and Creativity." She, two English profes-
    sors, and I, as a philosophy professor, taught this subject. Then in
    1991, at Eastern Connecticut State University, Professor Ellen
    Brodie and I co-taught a course on creativity.

8.   I am convinced that my housekeeper and friend, Mrs. Dolly Hendrick, is a psychic. Let me offer just one example to justify my belief. One day a piece of mail came from another friend who lived in Newport, Rhode Island. Dolly brought the piece of mail to me. She was not acquainted with the friend in Newport, as the friend in Newport and I had known one another in California, and we had both recently moved from California to different states in New England. Dolly walked into my study, and she asked me to feel her nose, which she said became ice-cold when she had a psychic experience. I felt her nose, and indeed it was ice-cold. Then, she told me that when she had picked up the envelope, the image which she had upon handling it was that of a murder in my friend's home. When I first visited my friend's new home in Newport, I told her of Dolly's image. My friend was astonished. Indeed, there had been a murder in her house that had taken place a number of years before.

9.   As with most Hindu literature, it is difficult to date an ancient text. However, as I noted in endnote #4, Sarvepalli Radhakrishnan and Charles Moore, editors of *A Sourcebook of Indian Philosophy*, p. 453, place Patañjali, the author of the *Yoga Sūtra*, as living during the second century BCE.

10.   In Book III, Verse 37, of the *Yoga Sūtra*, in a book entitled *The Yoga System of Patañjali*, tr. by James Haughton Woods, pp. 265-266, the explanation (Tattva Vaiśaradī of Vācaspati-Misra) makes clear that the yogin bent on self-realization cannot be attached to the perfections, i.e., intuition and power, which arise because of his advanced stage of discipline, etc. These perfections go counter to the attainment of that goal. In other words, the yogin must finally give up all knowledge of the world and power if he is to achieve self-realization.

WHY EXISTING VIEWS OF INTUITION HAVE BEEN REJECTED OR IGNORED?

As I stated in the Introduction to this book, from ancient times to the present, intuition is mentioned, discussed or implied, in a number of both Western and non-Western philosophical writings; however, accounts as to the nature of intuition, and how it functions, are not common. Nonetheless, there is what I take to be a traditional Western philosophical view of what intuition is. In addition to the traditional Western philosophical -view as to the nature of intuition, there is a traditional Hindu philosophical view of what intuition is which appears to predate the Western view by hundreds of years.[1]

In this chapter, I will focus on the traditional Western view, rather than Western philosophical writings which only allude to or mention some of the uses of intuition. Also, as I indicated in the Introduction, I will explore the Western non-traditional view of intuition found in the philosophy of Henri Bergson. This exploration is, in my view, a significant consideration, because intuition is central to Bergson's philosophy, and he does consider its nature. Finally, I will discuss the traditional Hindu view of intuition, as put forth in the ancient writing, the *Yoga Sūtra*, by Patañjali.[2]

After explicating the Western traditional philosophical account as to the nature of intuition, I will criticize the account because, according to it, intuition is taken to be a form of knowledge. I will argue that such a view disregards the nature of knowledge itself. To be more specific, I will argue that knowledge involves or is the result of reasoning, hence, it is discursive. Therefore, intuition cannot be a non-discursive form or independent way of gaining knowledge.

After considering the account of intuition in the philosophy of Henri Bergson, I will also criticize his account of it, because he too takes intuition to be a form of knowledge. In addition, I will identify several other problems with his philosophy. Finally, I will criticize the traditional Hindu view of intuition, according to which intuition is a higher form of knowledge, and in this context, I will again argue that intuition is not a form, even a higher form, of knowledge.

The Traditional View of Intuition in Western Philosophy

In my doctoral dissertation, entitled *Intuition as an Integral Process of the Mind*,[3] I noted that in an article on intuition in the *Encyclopedia of Philosophy*, Richard Rorty, the author, said that the broadest definition of the word "intuition" is immediate apprehension.[4] However, according to Rorty, "apprehension" is used to describe such disparate states as sensation, knowledge, and mystical rapport,[5] while "immediate" is used to signify the absence of: (1) causes, (2) the ability to define a term, (3) justification, (4) symbols, and (5) thought.[6] Because these terms have so many uses, Rorty despaired of finding a basic meaning of "immediate apprehension." I, however, sought the essential meaning of the term by observing the historical development of the word "intuition." The following is my account of the subject:

According to the *Oxford Universal Dictionary of the English Language*, the noun "intuition" is a French adoption of the late or medieval Latin word *intuitionem* which is a form of *intueri* which means to look.[7] In time, the word "intuition" came to mean: a looking into; inspection; a sight or view.[8]

By 1652, scholastic philosophers[9] took "intuition" to mean immediate knowledge.[10] However, this knowledge was ascribed to angelic and spiritual beings with whom vision and knowledge were held to be identical.[11]

As early as 1600, modern philosophers[12] took "intuition" to mean immediate apprehension by the mind without the intervention of any reasoning process; a particular act of such apprehension.[13] I take "modern philosophers" to be those philosophers belonging to the modern period of philosophy which followed the scholastic period, and preceded the recent period.

By 1659, "intuition" was used in the sense of immediate apprehension of the intellect alone; an act of such apprehension.[14]

By 1819, the word "intuition" was used in the sense of: immediate apprehension by sense; an act of such apprehension.[15]

Obviously, the key meaning of "intuition," for modern philosophers, was immediate apprehension. Furthermore, in the first definition of "intuition" ascribed to modern philosophers (1600), "immediate" clearly means direct, i.e., not mediated by the reasoning process. The second definition of "immediate" seems to retain this same meaning (1659). However, according to the second definition, it appears that apprehension is attributed to a faculty of the mind, i.e., the intellect. The last definition listed (1819) has to do with immediate apprehension by the sense or senses, i.e., sense perception. Regarding this last definition, since neither the traditional view of "intuition" which I am pursuing, nor my own view of what intuition is, are directly related to sense perception, I will leave the discussion of this subject until Chapter III when I consider certain epistemological views which limit the meaning of "intuition" to sense perception or what is given in sense experience.

Having determined that, in general, modern philosophers took "intuition" to mean immediate apprehension, and "immediate" meant not mediated by the reasoning process, and also that the scholastics took intuition to be immediate knowledge, although this knowledge was ascribed to spiritual beings rather than humans, I want to consider what the scholastics meant by "immediate knowledge." More specifically, I want to determine what the scholastics meant by "immediate," and if modern philosophers retained the scholastic meaning of "immediate" as it applied to intuition.

Furthermore, I want to explore the relation between "knowledge," used by the scholastics, and "apprehension" used by modern philosophers. With these questions in mind, I turn to a consideration of what the scholastics meant by "immediate knowledge."

Since the scholastics held that vision and knowledge were the same for angelic and spiritual beings to whom they attributed immediate knowledge, I take it that for these beings, to see was to know. Thus, what the scholastics seem to have meant by "knowledge," when they spoke of "immediate knowledge," was a recognition or grasp of what is real or true, and "immediate" seems clearly to have meant direct or sudden in that the grasp did not require the steps of reasoned inference. Hence, it seems to me that what the scholastics meant by "immediate knowledge" is a direct grasp or mental taking hold of, i.e., comprehension, which is not mediated by the reasoning process, of what is true or real.

Given what the scholastics and the modern philosophers meant by "immediate," it seems clear that the modern philosophers used the term in the same sense as the earlier scholastics, namely, non-mediated by the reasoning process. Now, keeping in mind what the scholastics meant by "knowledge," namely, the mental grasp of the true or real, I shall consider what modern philosophers seem to have meant by "apprehension," when speaking of "immediate apprehension."

In order to understand what modern philosophers meant by "apprehension," when speaking of "immediate apprehension," it may help to consider some dictionary definitions of "apprehension," i.e., mental apprehension. Five of the following definitions are listed in *The Oxford Universal Dictionary of the English Language*,[16] the sixth definition is listed in *The American Heritage Dictionary of the English Language*.[17]

1. the apprehensive faculty; understanding (1580).
2. the product or the abiding result of grasping mentally; a conception, a view, a notion, an opinion (1579).
3. sensible perception, arc. (1590).

4. the action of grasping with the intellect; conception; intellection (1597).
5. the action of learning (1641).
6. the ability to apprehend or understand; understanding (dictionary published in 1969).

Although the foregoing definitions include: a faculty, an action, an ability, as well as the product of an action, it seems to me that what modern philosophers usually meant by "apprehension," when they spoke of "immediate apprehension," is an action, namely, a mental grasp or grasping.

Based upon what has been said about "immediate" and "apprehension," I conclude that what modern philosophers usually meant by "immediate apprehension," is a mental grasp or grasping which is not mediated by the reasoning process.

Given the foregoing meaning of "immediate apprehension," and the meaning of "immediate knowledge," which the scholastics attributed to spiritual beings, namely, a mental grasp of the true or real which is not mediated by the reasoning process, it seems clear that the notion underlying each of these definitions of "intuition," is a mental grasp or grasping which is not mediated by the reasoning process. However, what I want to emphasize is that the grasp attributed to spiritual beings and the grasp made by human beings differ with respect to knowledge.

Setting aside any belief in spiritual beings, and focusing simply on human beings, it is the case that humans make errors in both perception and judgment, hence they need to be able to support their beliefs and justify their claims to knowledge. This support and justification involves reasoning, i.e., critical reasoning. Critical reasoning involves logical inference, and this, in turn, involves issues of evidence, credibility, coherence, consistency, etc. Therefore, I think that any rigorous thinker will agree that because knowledge involves reasoning, it is by its very nature discursive.

Given that knowledge is discursive, how can intuition, as non-discursive, be a form or independent way of gaining knowledge? Certainly, if a rigorous thinker were arguing with someone about a claim to knowledge, and that person stated that she/he had no reasons to support the claim, but, nonetheless, she/he knew it to be so, the rigorous thinker would not give any credence to the claim.

Focusing briefly on the broader subject of knowledge, I want to note how the development of epistemological considerations has, over the last few hundred years, changed the very enterprise of Western philosophy. In fact, the change from the scholastic period to the modern period of philosophical thought can be viewed as a response to the ever growing concern with epistemological considerations. To be more specific, as philosophers began to put more credence in science, mathematics, and logic, there was an ever increasing demand that claims to knowledge and theories of knowledge be supported by reasons which were justifiable. In time, there were even some philosophers who came to accept the scientific criterion that objective verifiability is required for claims to knowledge, i.e., justified beliefs.[18] The result of this epistemological thrust was that those beliefs which formed the foundation of the scholastic view of knowledge were questioned by an ever increasing number of philosophers. For those philosophers demanding objective verifiability, religious beliefs, in general, were meaningless. For those philosophers requiring justifiability independently of specific religious traditions or sacred texts, the religious beliefs of the scholastics seemed questionable at best. I will analyze the subject of justification of a belief in Chapter III.

The epistemological quest, mentioned above, has continued into the recent philosophical period, and it has culminated in the writings of a group of various thinkers who have in common the rejection of any certain knowledge about metaphysical structure. These thinkers are loosely labeled "post-modern" "post-structuralist," and "deconstructionist." The aforementioned rejection rests on the belief that there is no set structure to language, hence, language is a construct, and knowledge is confined within the fluid parameters of language. Some of these thinkers deny that there can be any general, let alone certain, knowledge of reality.[19] I will have more to say about this line of thinking in Chapter III, in which I will argue that these thinkers have ignored the use of intuition as a means to knowledge.

What I have argued in the foregoing discussion of knowledge, is that rigorous thinkers, the world over, take knowledge to be discursive, and such being the case, intuition cannot be a non-discursive form or independent way of gaining knowledge. The problem is that what I have described as the traditional Western philosophical view of the nature of intuition, namely, a non-discursive form or independent way of gaining knowledge, has continued to be the generally accepted notion of what intuition is within Western philosophical circles as well as other circles of thought. I contend that it is this view that has led many rigorous thinkers to either reject or ignore any consideration of intuition as part of the human experience. However, the problem that these thinkers face is what I explained earlier, namely, that without intuition, which I claim is a natural part of the mind's life, much of human experience is either inadequately explained, or cannot be explained.

Intuition in the Philosophy of Henri Bergson

Having set forth and criticized the traditional Western view as to the nature of intuition, I want to consider and analyse a non-traditional Western view of the subject which is found in the philosophy of Henri Bergson. Since intuition is central to Bergson's philosophy, and he did consider its nature and uses, I think that it is necessary to examine his account of the subject. However, as was the case with the traditional Western view of the subject, which I previously considered, in Bergson's philosophy, intuition is also taken to be a non-discursive form or independent way of gaining knowledge. I have argued that such a view is unacceptable to rigorous thinkers in general, because knowledge is taken to be discursive. Also, Bergson limited his notion of intuition to what

I take to be a use of one kind of intuition, which I identify as "creative insight." I will explain this insight in Chapter II. Finally, certain fundamental aspects of Bergson's metaphysics which he based on intuition, are in my view unwarranted.

The most complete account of intuition in Bergson's writings is to be found in *The Creative Mind: an Introduction to Metaphysics*. There, Bergson set forth his account as to the nature of intuition, and his metaphysics which is based on intuition. In order to appreciate what Bergson said about intuition, it is important to know that he contrasted intuition with what he called "intellect."[20] By "intellect," in general, Bergson seems to have meant reasoning, in the broad sense, including: memory, association of ideas, abstraction, analysis, generalization, interpretation and attention.[21] Also, what is characteristic of intellect, for Bergson, is that via intellect the world appears to be static. According to Bergson, it is as if intellect can only form pictures of what in reality is a process.[22]

Bergson held that humans can know that reality is a process only via intuition. In general, Bergson took intuition to be a non-mediated "seeing into"[23] by "an entering into" the flow of consciousness.[24] Also, although he sometimes spoke of intuition as a faculty,[25] a function,[26] and ". . . the attention the mind gives itself over and above its object. . .,"[27] he more often described it as a mental act or series of acts,[28] which can constitute a philosophical method.[29] Via intuition as an act or series thereof, Bergson held that one can directly participate in the immediacy of experience.[30] It is important to note that Bergson believed that knowledge gained via intuition, unlike knowledge gained via intellect, is precise, and attains absolute reality.[31]

Intuition, according to Bergson, is simple, by which he seemed to mean uncomplicated,[32] and yet it is also difficult as it involves considerable effort to detach oneself from the intellectual way of knowing.[33] When one is able to detach herself/himself from the intellect, and employ intuition, she/he enters into what Bergson speaks of as "the current of direct awareness,"[34] "the stream of one's own consciousness,"[35] or "the flow of one's inner life."[36]

Bergson called this flowing of one's personality through time "duration" (*duree*). He said of this duration that it is: (1) a heterogeneous flux or becoming; (2) irreversible — straining towards the future; (3) continually creating nearness or novelty, hence intrinsically unpredictable; (4) an inexhaustible source of freedom; and (5) its living reality can never be communicated by images or concepts, but must be directly intuited.[37] As conveyed in the fifth definition of duration, Bergson held that only via intuition can one know of duration. Such knowledge cannot be gained via the intellect or reasoning.[38]

In addition to the foregoing definitions of duration, Bergson's descriptions of it, quoted below, make clear that it is a conscious process of the mind involving memory, whereby the past survives in the present and affects the present: ". . . there is no mood, however simple, which does not change every moment, since there is no consciousness without memory, and no continuation of a state without the addition, to the present feeling, of the memory of past moments. This is what duration consists of."[39] "Inner duration is the continuous life of a memory which prolongs the past into the present..."[40]

Once one is able to intuit her/his own inner duration, Bergson believed that she/he can intuit or be brought in contact with a whole continuity of durations.[41] Based on this intuition or contact, Bergson suggested that there can be a broader sense of duration which he takes to be a synthesis of conscious moments bound together in a unity.[42] Unity, according to Bergson, "will appear as some immobile substance, or some intemporal substratum of that which is moving."[43] At one point, Bergson likened this unity to an eternity of life.[44]

It is not just duration itself which Bergson believed that humans intuit. He held that humans intuit a vital impulse (*élan vital*). The vital impulse is more fundamental than duration, but apparently it encompasses duration.[45] According to Bergson, this vital impulse drives life or nature towards

ever higher levels of organization.[46] Bergson also suggested
that the vital impulse is the basic cause of the variations which
produce new species, and even the principle of life in general.[47]

Based on certain remarks which Bergson made about intuition, and the vital impulse, it seems clear that he believed
that a description of the vital impulse is limited to analogies
and metaphors.[48] In fact, he offered the following analogy of
the vital impulse and a jet of steam. He described the vital
impulse as "a jet of steam spurting into the air continually,
condensing into myriads of drops, and falling back to the
source. The drops represent the purely material aspect of the
universe against which life wages a ceaseless battle. At the
summit of the jet, where a small part of the steam remains
uncondensed for some seconds, we have the analogue of the
living species thrown up by evolution."[49]

The foregoing description of the vital impulse reminds one
somewhat of Heidegger's notion of the coming forth of Being
(*ereignis*)[50] which could be likened to a fountain that never
turns off,[51] and the idea that each human being as the place
where Being is revealed (Dasein)[52] is at some time a part of
the coming forth of Being, and then she/he dies, hence,
drops out.[53]

In Bergson's work, *Creative Evolution*, he spoke of a source
or origin of the vital impulse.[54] He referred to this source
as a supra consciousness,[55] and he even suggested that the
term "God" could be used for the source from which all things
flow. In his *Two Sources of Morality and Religion*, Bergson again
spoke of a primal energy at the heart of the universe. He
likened this energy to love.[56] Also, as one Bergsonian scholar
notes, Bergson accepted the Christian mystic's view that God
is love, and the object of love.[57] Bergson contended that "this
truth [the truth that God is love] is certified by intuition when
it rises to the heights of mystical experience where union with
the Divine is achieved."[58]

Having set forth Bergson's view as to the nature of intuition, and considered certain fundamental aspects of his

metaphysics, which he held were gained via intuition, I want to return to the critique which I mentioned when I introduced this topic. As I made clear at that time, I disagree with Bergson's view that intuition is a non-discursive form or independent way of gaining knowledge. As I have stated in this chapter, and will argue in Chapter II, I take intuition to be only one means to knowledge which needs to be checked by reason. Also, as I will make clear when I explain the two forms of intuition which I have identified, I take Bergson's intuition into the inner duration of the self to be basically one form of the kind of intuition which I call "creative insight." Regarding Bergson's claims about the metaphysics of duration, in general, and the vital force, I hold that they are unwarranted because the claims cannot be verified. Furthermore, the belief in a vital force is at odds with other accounts of reality, e.g., a Hindu account, which I will explain in Chapter V, of an unchanging all pervasive state of consciousness and bliss which underlies all change and flux. As I shall suggest in this last chapter of this book, at this point in time, humans cannot speak with any conviction about the nature of the Ultimate.

To summarize my view of Bergson's account of the nature of intuition, I take it to be one form of a particular kind of intuition which I call "creative insight." As to Bergson's metaphysics or ontology, which he claimed was gained directly by intuition, I accept his account of a person's inner duration, but not his account of duration in general or of the vital impulse.

The Traditional View of Intuition in Hindu Philosophy

Having set forth the Traditional Western view, and a non-Traditional Western view, of intuition, let us consider the Traditional View of Intuition in the Hindu philosophical tradition. What I take to be the traditional view of intuition in Hindu philosophy has its source in the account of intuition found in the *Yoga Sūtra* of Patañjali. As I explained in the Introduction, the *Yoga Sūtra* of Patañjali set forth the basic tenets of the Yoga school of philosophy which was established about two thousand years ago, but it has roots which are much earlier. A sūtra (literally meaning thread) is an aphorism. Traditionally, the basic text for a philosophical system consisted of a set of aphorisms setting forth the leading concepts and doctrines of the system concerned.[59] However, since the Yoga school was focused upon achieving self-realization, the *Yoga Sūtra* was primarily a guide to the moral, physical and mental disciplines that the yogins, i.e., the followers of Patañjali's Yoga school of philosophy, had to master in order to achieve self-realization. I will consider what the yogins took to be self-realization shortly.

It was Patañjali who set forth the philosophical view of intuition as a supra-normal insight, although the source of this belief is ancient.[60] According to Patañjali, this supra-normal insight comes about only when one has mastered the moral, physical and mental disciplines set forth in the *Yoga Sūtra*.

In order to understand what Patañjali says about intuition, we need to consider certain aspects of the philosophy of the Yoga school. However, even a rudimentary understanding of the Yoga school of philosophy requires an awareness of the source of Hindu philosophical thought, the various Hindu schools of philosophy, and some of the general beliefs of the Hindus.

In an attempt to address the foregoing requirements for an understanding of the Yoga school of philosophy, I will adumbrate some of the basic history concerning the source of Hindu philosophical thought, the Hindu schools of philosophy, and some shared general beliefs of the Hindus.

Although the term *Hindu* has a popular usage,[61] in a philosophical context, it refers to those schools of philosophy, which I shall mention shortly, taken by the Hindus to be orthodox in that they accept the authority of the *Vedas*, i.e., the sacred scriptures of the Hindus. The unorthodox schools include Indian Buddhism, Jainism, and Cārvāka. The *Vedas* express the myth of the Hindu people. By "myth," I mean the sacred story of a people, true and/or fictional (actually, almost always both), embracing their most fundamental beliefs and values. The *Vedas* are divided into four books. Also, even though the first sections of the books deal with subjects such as insights into the origin and nature of reality, rituals, rites, sacrifices, etc., the latter part of the books, called the *Upaniṣads* (literally, to sit by devotedly)[62] consist of writings which are more philosophic in nature. Although dating within the Hindu tradition is imprecise at best,[63] the first book of the *Vedas*, namely The *Ṛg Veda* (pronounced *Rig Veda*) is taken to be at least 1500 years old.[64]

Each of the Hindu schools of philosophy has roots in the *Vedas*, however, they arose over a period of many hundreds of years, and some are taken to be older than others. Some scholars hold that the earliest school, namely, Sāṅkhya, began about the 7th century B.C.[65] Originally, there were six schools of Hindu philosophy: Sāṅkhya, Yoga, Pūrva Mīmāṁsā, Nyāya, Vaiśeṣika, and Vedānta. Sāṅkhya is basically a dualistic metaphysics. Yoga adopted the metaphysics of Sāṅkhya to a great extent (I shall have more to say about this shortly.) when the two schools joined. However, Yoga is focused on self-realization and the discipline required to achieve self-realization. The early Pūrva Mīmāṁsā school is focused on an exegesis of the Vedic texts.[66] Nyāya has to do with logic and epistemology. Vaiśeṣika, which joined with the Nyāya school, is fundamentally an atomistic metaphysics. Vedānta is a metaphysics of unity based on an interpretation of the Upaniṣads.[67]

At the present time, Vedānta seems to be the only school which is vital,[68] and indeed one of its branches, Advaita Vedānta, is pervasive in Hindu thought.[69] However, there is an increasing interest in Nyāya by a number of Western and comparative philosophers. Part of the reason for the interest may be that as a methodology, both of logic and epistemology, Nyāya influenced not only the other schools of Hindu philosophy, but also certain Buddhist schools which debated the conclusions of the Nyāya logicians.[70]

With regard to yoga, as a discipline involving moral, physical and ultimately mental constraints, it has continued to form a part of the "yogas" or paths to realization, which I will discuss shortly.

Having only mentioned the Hindu schools of philosophy and the major focus of concern for each school, let me turn to some of the general themes of Hinduism which are necessary in order to understand what I will say about the Yoga school of philosophy. What I take to be the most fundamental belief in the Hindu tradition can be broadly classified as the karmic law. However, as we shall see, dharma, i.e., basically duty, as the force which moves the "karmic wheel of life," is an integral part of the karmic law. The karmic law can be described as a cosmic law involving order and justice. However, the law applies to each individual who, through a process of self-development, can, over a period of many lifetimes, achieve self-realization, and thereby, mokṣa, i.e., release from saṁsāra, i.e., the continuing cycles of rebirth.

In order to understand the Hindu desire for release, one must internalize the fact that in general, Hindus view life as a state of suffering. Hence, the objective is to end that suffering by a release from the cycles of rebirth. However, the cycles will not cease until one achieves self-realization. What constitutes self-realization differs with the various Hindu schools of philosophy. However, speaking in broad generalities, one can say that each person or self has to go through a process of development which involves overcoming the ego-self. Furthermore, each person is bound or fettered by those qualities carried forth from her or his earlier life and past lives. To say that one is bound or fettered does not mean that one cannot break the bonds, otherwise change and development would be impossible. However, most change is brought about by great effort. Nevertheless, in order to progress towards self-realization, one must break the "shackles" from the past. Furthermore, the progress or decline of a person within a given lifetime determines the state of life that she or he will encounter in the next lifetime.

An appealing part of the belief in karma, i.e., the karmic law, is that there are many chances to improve one's character and knowledge. However, the belief that whatever condition one finds herself/himself in is the result of one's past behavior simply strikes some non-Hindus as wrong and/or unacceptable. For example, how can one hold that a child with some infirmity, such as my deceased nephew, who was born brain damaged, is responsible for the psychic pain which he experienced both in and out of mental institutions.[71] There are many such examples which give non-Hindus pause when considering the karmic law as a fundamental belief and not just an academic study. However, from a Hindu perspective, it is the law of karma which keeps order, harmony, and justice, as each self continues through many lifetimes, some progressing towards self-realization, some not, and some even regressing to a lower stage of development. There is no release from this process until and unless one achieves self-realization.

The basic force which propels one forward or backward in the life cycles is dharma. The term *dharma* has many meanings, e.g., to uphold, justice, righteousness, etc., however, the most common meaning seems to be duty.[72] Each person has duties in a given lifetime. Unfortunately, the traditional view concerning one's duties has been associated with one's caste. As is well-known, the caste system, though not specifically grounded in Vedic literature,[73] has a long history in the Indian society or culture. Traditionally, the four *varnas* or classes have been viewed as castes. They are: brāhmaṇa, i.e., priest; kṣatriya, i.e. warrior; vaiśya, i.e., merchant; and sūdra. i.e., serf. Obviously, these are stratified from the highest rank, which is the brāhmaṇa, to the lowest, which is the sūdra, but they are also viewed as reflecting a person's level of karmic development. It is the brāhman who is taken to be highly developed and far along the path to self-realization. Over time, there have arisen different classifications of the varnas and many distinctions as to the subclasses of the varnas. However, what is important for the subject at issue, is that one's dharma or duties in life are held to be determined by one's caste. If one does not perform her or his dharma, it is believed that she/he will not progress in her/ his karmic development. Furthermore, as I have indicated, because of certain actions, it is possible to regress to a lower stage of development.

Based on what I have said about castes, one needs to note that caste is established by birth, and traditionally persons have married within their given castes. This being the case, from the perspective of one lifetime, a person's lot in life is determined by one's birth. However, the Hindus believe that if one has performed her/his dharma, then she/he can hope and expect to be born into a family of a higher caste in some future lifetime. Thus, one in the lowest caste can still aspire to a better lot in a future lifetime, and, more importantly, develop towards self-realization. Given such a class structure, the abuses of oppression are obvious. However, it is interesting that in the present Hindu society a vaiśya is sometimes a person of means, and a brāhmaṇa is a servant. Having touched upon the doctrines of karma and dharma, I want to consider another general theme which is germane to what I will say about the Yoga school of philosophy, namely, the various paths, called *yogas*, to mokṣa, i.e., release from saṁsāra, i.e. future rebirths. Basically, they are bhakti yoga which has to do with devotion; karma yoga, which has to do with good works; and jñāna yoga, which has to do with knowledge, especially what is viewed as a higher spiritual form of knowledge. This knowledge is a kind of intuition which presupposes higher reasoning powers and moral development....[74] Also, although it is sometimes categorized as a separate yoga, yoga discipline involving meditation is actually a part of each of these paths.[75]

A third general theme of Hindu thought has to do with āśramas or stages of development for a given individual. Briefly, the first is a student stage wherein one learns from her or his guru or teacher. Next is the householder stage wherein one takes on the family life, enjoys the sensual pleasures of marriage, material pursuits, has children, etc.

When one has satisfied the desires and duties attending to this stage, one enters what is called the "forest dweller" stage of development. This stage can take a number of lifetimes to reach. At this stage one loses interest in worldly gains and sensual pleasures. He becomes more detached from the desire for things or experiences. (I use the term "he" because, traditionally, it has been only the male who could aspire to the higher stages. However, there is no inconsistency in the belief that one can change gender from one lifetime to another.)[76] He finds himself becoming more contemplative and needing solitude for his spiritual quest. The last stage which takes many lifetimes to reach, is that of a sannyāsa or holy person. The life of a sannyāsa has traditionally been one of an ascetic who is focused on meditation and via that meditation, achieves self-realization. Within this stage are persons ranging from one who has seriously undertaken a spiritual or holy life to the person who has achieved self-realization.[77]

Having set forth those Hindu themes which I take to be essential for an understanding of the Yoga school of philosophy which is set forth in Patañjali's *Yoga Sūtra*, let me very briefly highlight the features of the school which are necessary in order to understand Patañjali's view of intuition as a supranormal insight. As I argue in an article which I wrote on the subject, the metaphysics of Patañjali's Yoga school represents a shift away from the strict dualism of the earlier Sāṅkhya school which Yoga is said to have adopted when it joined with Sāṅkhya.[78] However, for the purposes at hand, I will only introduce some aspects of the Sāṅkhya metaphysics, and offer a few comments as to some of the differences between the Yoga and Sāṅkhya metaphysics. Very briefly, according to the Sāṅkhya metaphysics, there are two distinct aspects of reality, one material, and one nonmaterial. The material aspect of reality is taken to be the physical world which includes even the human mind. This material world is comprised of constituents called *guṇas*. (This material world is often referred to as *Prakṛti*.)[79] Within the material world, the guṇas can be classified as follows:

sattva — i.e., that which is light, as opposed to dark, and buoyant; also that which is illuminating
rajas — i.e., energy, force, or power
tamas — i.e., that which resists energy, is associated with inertia, and that which is dark and/or heavy

While the material aspect of reality is comprised of the guṇas, the nonmaterial aspect is made up of separate states of pure consciousness. The question of what would constitute a separate state of pure consciousness was and is an insolvable problem, as far as I am concerned.[80] However, it is important to recognize that in the Sāṅkhya school, consciousness is not the collective all pervasive state of reality called *Brahman* which underlies· the physical world. (This view of an all pervasive consciousness is found in the Vedic literature, and, as I shall explain, in Chapter V, in the Advaita Vedānta school of philosophy.) According to the Sāṅkhya school, pure consciousness called Puruṣa, is comprised of a plurality of conscious states of being which are inactive. It would seem that for every material self, or the traces of that self in a process of transmigration, there is a corresponding Puruṣa. In order to achieve release from the cycles of rebirth, which I spoke of earlier, the Sāṅkhya school held that, via a process of evolution (which I will not consider, as it is not necessary for the purpose at hand), one must come to realize that there are two aspects of reality, namely, Puruṣa, and the material world of the guṇas (technically called *prakṛti* when the guṇas are in equipoise),[81] and they are distinct.

As I mentioned earlier, the Yoga school is said to have adopted the Sāṅkhya metaphysics when the two schools merged. However, the Yoga school, unlike the Sāṅkhya school, expressed a belief in a God, even though, what the yogins call *Īśvara*, i.e., Lord or God, was actually a state of Puruṣa which was never subject to the cycles of rebirth. Also, as I mentioned earlier, there was a shift from the strict dualistic metaphysics of the Sāṅkhya school, according to which Puruṣa and the material world were both equally real. Unlike the Sāṅkhya school, the Yoga school adopted a hierarchical view according to which the states of Puruṣa were more real than the material world of the guṇas. Furthermore, those Yogins who in their karmic development could master the moral, physical and spiritual discipline, could then undertake yoga proper, i.e., the mental discipline required to still the fluctuations of the mind caused by the guṇas of the material world. Only via yoga proper, i.e., the stilling of the mind, could one hope to realize Puruṣa as the true self. I will discuss yoga proper in Chapter V.

With this sketch of the Yoga metaphysics, one can begin to appreciate Patañjali's view that intuition is a supranormal insight. According to Patañjali, when a yogin develops yoga proper, i.e., the stilling of the mind, to a high state called *saṁyama*, which I will explain in Chapter V, intuition arises. However, it arises by stages. Actually what transpires is that consciousness is shinning ever more brightly into an unconscious material world. In Hindu terms, one speaks of self-luminosity or self-revelation. It is as if the true self were a light or torch which when unobscured could illumine the entire universe, and via that light, one could see into all aspects of reality. Given the foregoing view, it is clear that, for Patañjali, intuition is a supra-normal insight by which one gains knowledge of reality.

The view that intuition is a supra-normal insight giving one knowledge of reality was shared by the Vedānta school, with some modifications,[82] which will become clearer when I consider the Advaita Vedānta tradition in Chapter V, and it was at least recognized by the Nyāya school.[83] However, as I mentioned earlier, these schools differed with Yoga as to the nature of reality.

With regard to the traditional Hindu view of the nature of intuition, as adumbrated above, according to which intuition is a higher form of knowledge, I level the same criticism

as that which I gave of the traditional Western view of the
subject, and Henri Bergson's view. Recall that when criticizing
the Western view, I argued that knowledge by its very nature
is discursive. Such being the case, because human beings
make errors in perception and judgment, they need to engage
in critical reasoning. Critical reasoning involves logical inference, and this, in turn, involves issues of evidence, credibility,
coherence, consistency, etc. Thus, when one makes a claim
to knowledge, she or he is expected to give reasons for that
claim if asked to do so. Those reasons have to be good and
sufficient to warrant the inference to the conclusion. "Good"
unpacks as: true or factual or reasonable to accept, and
relevant. I will say more about this subject in Chapter III,
when I discuss knowledge in more depth. However, I think
it is clear that knowledge involves reasoning, and, hence, it
makes no sense to speak of intuition as a non-discursive form
or independent way of gaining knowledge. What does make
sense, as I will argue in Chapter II, is that intuition is one
means to knowledge. Furthermore, as I will make clear,
intuition is complementary to and can by checked by reason.

I will have more to say about my views regarding the
traditional Hindu view of intuition as self-luminosity or self-
revelation in Chapter V. For the present, let me just say that
certainly intuition with regard to the self enables one to gain
insight into the self, and even gain some inklings as to the
meaning of life. However, again I level the criticism that
intuition is not knowledge, but only one means to knowledge.
Hence, I would argue that for yogins, or any human beings,
insight is not to be equated with knowledge. Nevertheless,
I will argue that via insight the limits of knowledge can be
expanded greatly. As I will explain in Chapter II, I think that
knowledge is the result of sense experience, intuition, reason,
and revelation (again, revelation in the Heideggerian sense
of what is presented in experience).

ENDNOTES

1. If, as I stated earlier (in endnote #4 of the Introduction), we date the traditional Hindu view of Patañjali at about the second century B.C., and the traditional Western view sometime during the scholastic period (W.L. Reese, in a (*Dictionary of Philosophy,* said that some people would date the beginning of the scholastic period in the 7th century A.D., and extend it to the 15th century A.D. However, as he noted, its height was about the 12th or 13th centuries A.D.), the traditional Hindu view predates the scholastic view by hundreds of years.

2. Again, as I noted in endnote #4 of the Introduction to this book, Patañjali lived and wrote the *Yoga Sūtra* sometime during the second century B.C.

3. A Dissertation submitted to the Faculty of Claremont Graduate School in partial fulfillment of the requirements for the degree of Doctor of Philosophy in the Graduate Faculty of Individual Degrees (sub-field — East-West Comparative Philosophy).

4. Richard Rorty, "Intuition" in *The Encyclopedia of Philosophy,* vol. 4, p. 204.

5. *Ibid.*

6. *Ibid.*

7. *The Oxford Universal Dictionary.*

8. *Ibid.*

9. The scholastic philosophers held to a system of theological and philosophical teachings which predominated in the high middle ages. These teachings were based on the authority of the Latin Fathers and of Aristotle and his commentators.

10. *The Oxford Universal Dictionary.*

11. *Ibid.*

12. *Ibid.* I take "modern philosopher," in this context, to mean those philosophers who, unlike the scholastics, did not base their views and theories on church authority. This is not to say that some of their views were not influenced by church doctrine. René Descartes is usually said to be the father of the modern period of philosophy, although he was not born until 1596.

13. *The Oxford Universal Dictionary.*

14. *Ibid.*

15. *Ibid.*

16. *Ibid.*

17. *The American Heritage Dictionary of the English Language.*
18. *The Dictionary of Philosophy and Religion*, by W. L. Reese: The verifiability criterion derived from a theory of meaning elaborated initially in the Vienna Circle of Logical Positivists. The verifiability of a sentence or proposition is regarded as a necessary condition of its having meaning.
19. Included in these thinkers would be Richard Rorty and Michel Foucault.
20. *The Creative Mind: An Introduction to Metaphysics*, by Henri Bergson, Chapter I, pp. 30-31, and Chapter II, especially pp. 78–81.
21. *Ibid.*, pp. 16–17, 30–31, 34–35, 39–42, 75, 172–175; and Henri Bergson, *The Two Sources of Morality and Religion*, p. 46.
22. Henri Bergson, *The Creative Mind: An Introduction to Metaphysics*, pp. 16–17.
23. *Ibid.* pp. 13–14, 32–42, 159.
24. *Ibid.*, pp. 29, 159, and 187.
25. *Ibid.*, p. 199.
26. *Ibid.*, pp. 34 and179.
27. *Ibid.*, pp. 178-179.
28. Henri Bergson, *The Creative Mind: An Introduction to Metaphysics*, pp. 31, 35, 184 and 190; and the essay "An Introduction to Metaphysics," by Henri Bergson, tr. by T. E. Hulme, pp. 46–47.
29. *The Creative Mind: An Introduction to Metaphysics*, pp. 37, 107–129.
30. *Ibid.*, pp. 31–35, and 127–128.
31. *Ibid.*, pp. 29, 31–32, 159–162, 169, 192.
32. *Ibid.*, pp. 19, 108–109.
33. *Ibid.*, pp. 35, 190.
34. *Ibid.*, pp. 32, 34–35, and 42.
35. *Ibid.*
36. *Ibid.*, pp. 87, 187, 200.
37. *Ibid.*, pp. 16–20, and 34–35.
38. *Ibid.*, pp. 16–29.
39. *Ibid.*, p. 179.
40. *Ibid.*
41. *Ibid.*, pp. 184–189.
42. *Ibid.*, pp. 184–185.
43. *Ibid.*, p. 186.
44. *Ibid.*, p. 187.
45. *Ibid.*, pp. 199; also the essay "An Introduction to Metaphysics," tr. by T. E. Hulme, p. 47.

46. Henri Bergson, *Creative Mind: An Introduction to Metaphysics*, p. 199; also the essay "An Introduction to Metaphysics," tr. by T. E. Hulme, p. 17.

47. Henri Bergson, *The Two Sources of Morality and Religion*, p. 250.

48. Henri Bergson, *The Creative Mind: An Introduction to Metaphysics*, p. 42; and the essay "An Introduction to Metaphysics, by Henri Bergson, tr. by T. E. Hulme. p. 17.

49. Thomas A. Goudge, Editor's Introduction to the essay "An Introduction to Metaphysics," by Henri Bergson, tr. by T. E. Hulme, p. 17.

50. Martin Heidegger, *Being and Time*, pp. 433, and 440–441.; *The New Cassell's German Dictionary* by Funk and Wagnall, p. 136.

51. Hope Fitz, "The Mystical Experience From a Heideggerian Perspective," p. 51.

52. Martin Heidegger, *Being and Time*, pp. 332–335.

53. Fitz, "The Mystical Experience From a Heideggerian Perspective," p. 51.

54. Henry Bergson, *Creative Evolution*, tr. by Arthur Mitchell, p 87.

55. *Ibid.*

56. Henri Bergson, *The Two Sources of Morality and Religion*, p. 96.

57. Thomas a Goudge, Editor's Introduction to the essay "An Introduction to Metaphysics," by Henri Bergson, p. 19.

58. *Ibid.*, p. 261.

59. These tersely phrased statements were such that only the members of the school, at the time when the work was written, could understand them without some commentary. So through time, there have developed commentaries, and commentaries on the commentaries.

60. The insights of the seers in the ancient *Vedic* hymns such as the "Creation Hymn" (*Nāsadīya*) *Ṛg Veda*, 10.129, or "The Hymn to Man" (*Puruṣa-Sūkta*), *Ṛg Veda*, 10.90, certainly involved this kind of supra-normal insight.

61. The more popular use of the term *Hindu* conveys some of the beliefs and values which pervade much of Indian philosophy and life. Hindu thought, or Hinduism, in this more popular sense, may be described as that diverse body of religion, philosophy, and culture which is broadly characterized by a belief in reincarnation; a belief in a Supreme Being. Traditionally, there were three personifications of the Supreme Being, namely Brahma, Visnu, and Śiva. However, today only Visnu, in his many incarnations, and Śiva

are widely worshipped (along with the consorts who are often described as feminine aspects of the Gods, and a pantheon of lesser deities); and a desire for liberation from earthly evils.

62. John Grimes, *A Concise Dictionary of Indian Philosophy* (Sanskrit/ English).

63. Perhaps, the inattention to dating in ancient times is due, in part, to the cyclical view of life.

64. Most text books, with which I am familiar, state 1500 B.C., however, as Pandit Rajmani Tigunait, Ph.D. says in his book, *Seven Systems of Indian Philosophy*, the oral transmission of the *Vedas* could be as early as 4000 B.C.

65. In *A Sourcebook of Indian Philosophy*, the editors, Sarvepalli Radhakrishnan and Charles Moore, say that the authorship of the Sāṅkhya system of philosophy is ascribed to Kapila, who probably lived in the seventh century B.C.

66. As Pandit Rajmani Tegunait, Ph.D. states in the *Seven Systems of Indian Philosophy*, p. 183, the word *mīmāṁsā* means to analyze and understand thoroughly. Also, while the term *pūrva mīmāṁsā*, which refers to the early or initial teachings, was applied to the school which was based on determining one's dharma (including rituals, rites, etc.), from the *Vedic* texts; the term *uttara mīmāṁsā*, which refers to later or high teachings, was used in reference to the Vedānta school.

67. Advaita Vedānta, the non-dual school of Śaṅkara, involves a view of a strict unity of reality; Viśiṣṭādvaita, the modified non-dual school of Rāmānuja, still adheres to a unity of reality. However, I fail to see how Madhva's Dvaita school involving a view of a dual reality can be seen as unified.

68. It seems to me that Rāmānuja's Viśiṣṭādvaita school is of more interest than it used to be. Perhaps this is because of the belief, expressed in his writings, that Brahman is akin to what Śaṅkara called *Saguṇa Brahman*, i.e., Brahman with qualities, hence Īśvara, i.e., Lord or God. As such, the ultimate is not simply the impersonal absolute which Śaṅkara called *Nirguṇa Brahman*. This is not to say that one does not experience the absolute as the all pervasive state of consciousness and bliss, which I mention in Chapter V, but rather that Brahman is viewed as a kind of soul of reality which has as its body material things and selves.

69. I often think that if one had not studied the Hindu schools of philosophy, the impressions which one would have on her or his

first visit to India is that Advaita Vedānta is *the* Hindu philosophy of India.

70. Udayana, the great 12th century Nyāya logician, was engaged in debate with early Buddhist thinkers, in part, about the subject of the momentariness of reality.

71. My nephew, David Kittell, was not retarded, and he was well aware that he was different from other persons. He knew that he did not "fit" anywhere. Once he told me that if he could speak to God, he would tell Him a thing or two. I took that to mean that he did not think that he had been given a "fair shake."

72. Grimes, *A Concise Dictionary of Indian Philosophy, Dharma* — literally, "what holds together," and thus, it is the basis of all order, whether social or moral. As an ethical or moral value, it is the instrumental value to liberation (except for the Mīmāṁsāka who consider it the supreme value).

73. In the ancient "Hymn to Man" (Puruṣa — Sūkta), *Ṛg Veda*, 10.90, there is the division of cosmic man into classes, but that does not entail a caste system.

74. This very common Hindu view can be traced to the *Yoga Sūtra* of Patañjali (which I will consider in Chapter V), wherein intuition arises only after one has mastered yoga proper, i.e., mental discipline, which, in turn, is based on moral, spiritual, and physical discipline.

75. In Huston Smith's famous book, *The Religions of Man*, p. 51, there is a description of raja yoga, involving meditation, which seems to be a separate yoga path. However, in general, Hindus simply view meditation or what is called "yoga proper" in the *Yoga Sūtra* as part of karma yoga, bhakti yoga, or jñāna yoga.

76. It may be that women were viewed as lesser beings, and, as such, were simply not considered as being capable of achieving self-realization. However, I am not aware of any *Vedic* literature concerning rebirth wherein one is confined to a particular gender. Hence, the thinking of the ancients may well have been that one changes gender before aspiring to higher āśramas.

77. I think that this long arduous process is best described in the *Yoga Sūtra*.

78. Hope Fitz, "The Nature and Significance of Intuition in Patañjali's *Yoga Sūtra* and in the Philosophical Writings of Radhakrishnan," in *The Journal of Religious Studies*, Patiala [Punjab] India, Punjabi University, Vol. xxvi, Nos. 1 & 2, Spring-Autumn, 1995, pp. 10-12.

79. Even though the term *prakṛti*, i.e., primal matter, is sometimes used in reference to the material world, technically it is when the guṇas are in a dynamic state of equipoise or equilibrium. (Please see *Fundamentals of Indian Philosophy*, by Ramakrishnan Puligandala, p.122). This state occurs before and after a state of evolution. As I made clear in the text, I do not want to explain evolution in this book, as it is not directly germane to my subject. However, very briefly, before evolution (which must apply to an individual in a process of self-realization), the guṇas are in a state of equipoise (prakṛti). After evolution starts, they are out of balance. Also, after one has achieved self-realization (which in the Sāṅkhya and Yoga schools means that one has realized the dual nature of reality which is comprised of Puruṣa and the guṇas of the material world, and that both are distinct), one is thereby released from rebirth. After releasement, one exists in a state of kaivalya In this state there is Puruṣa and Prakṛti, i.e., the guṇas in a state of equipoise, and one will never be subject again to rebirth.

80. Perhaps the separate states of consciousness could be likened to monads of sorts, but what would constitute or establish the boundaries of a given state of consciousness?

81. Please see endnote number 79.

82. Since Vedāntins believe in the unity of reality, and that Ātman, i.e., the true self is veiled or obscured by māyā, i.e., illusion, then, in general, intuition is viewed not only as a higher form of knowledge, and a method of knowing (jñāna yoga), but also as the final insight involved in the realization of Ātman, and that Ātman is Brahman.

83. I find it fascinating that a school of logic and epistemology would accept a belief in extraordinary perception, including the supranormal perception of the yogins, which includes perception of: things or events in past lives or the future, as well as the present; what is hidden or concealed; or what is infinitely small in size. Obviously, these thinkers who relied on sense experience and reason for ordinary perception, did not rule out intuition and revelation for extraordinary perception.

CHAPTER II

THE NATURE AND KINDS OF INTUITION

Having set forth the traditional and a non-traditional Western view as to the nature of intuition, and a traditional Hindu view of the subject, and shown why these views are not acceptable to rigorous thinkers, I shall now set forth an account of the nature and kinds of intuition which can be accepted by rigorous thinkers the world over.

As I stated in the Introduction and Chapter I of this book, I am indebted to Sarvepalli Radhakrishnan for the core idea of intuition which I culled from his writings, and which inspired the line of thought that I follow in this book.[1] However, as I mentioned, Radhakrishnan held that intuition is a higher form of knowledge, and one that is gained independently of reason, while I argue that knowledge, by its very nature, is discursive, hence intuition cannot be a non-discursive form or independent way of gaining knowledge. As I have claimed, and will argue, I do hold that intuition is *one* means to knowledge. Also, I will introduce two kinds of intuition which are never identified as such in Radhakrishnan's works (or in any other work of which I am aware).[2] Finally, I will make clear that one must develop one's intuitive powers, just as one must develop one's intellectual powers.

Let us turn now to the core idea of intuition which I culled from Radhakrishnan's writings. Radhakrishnan used "intuition" in both a loose and a strict sense of a process of awareness. In a loose sense, Radhakrishnan spoke of intuition as any cognitive process of awareness which is direct or immediate in contrast to what is inferential, that is, mediated by the reasoning process.[3] He included both perceptual knowledge and what he called "integral insight" in the fore-going sense of intuition.[4] In a strict sense, Radhakrishnan confined "intuition" to integral insight.[5] It is Radhakrishnan's views concerning integral insight which I want to explicate.

Although Radhakrishnan neither defined nor clearly ex-plained what he meant by "integral insight," he did describe aspects of an integral process involved in integral insight. Also, as I shall explain, since his description of the process and the insight itself differ, it seems that he thought that the process culminated in an act of insight. In contrast to per-ception, which is usually viewed as the passive acceptance of observed data, the integral process is described as one in which the mind is actively engaged.[6] The following descrip-tions of the integral process are some of the most informative descriptions which Radhakrishnan offered on the subject:

> When intuition is defined as integral insight, the suggestion is that the whole mind is at work on it. Any coherent philosophy should take into account observed data, rational reflection, and intuitive insight.[7]
>
> In intuitive knowledge, man ceases to be an impartial spectator. His whole being is at work, not merely the powers of observation and inference.[8]
>
> Intuition is not used as an apology for doctrines which either could not or would not be justified on intellectual grounds. It is not shadowy sentiment or pathological fancy fit for cranks . . . . It stands to intellect as a whole to a part, as the creative source of thought to the created categories which act more or less automatically . . . . The different energies of the human soul are not cut off from one another by any impossible barriers. They flow into each other, modify, support, and control each other. The Sanskrit expression "Samyagdarsana" or in-tegral insight brings out how far away it is from occult visions, trance, and ecstasy.[9]

It seems to me that the first thing to notice about the

foregoing descriptions is that the integral process is characterized as a process of awareness in which the whole mind is at work.[10] It seems clear from what Radhakrishnan said, that the process involves perception and conceptual activities.[11] Obviously, the conceptual activities include the formation of concepts[12] and memory.[13] Radhakrishnan even suggested that the powers of inference form part of the process.[14] However, elsewhere he stated that the integral insight is a non-inferential process.[15] As I shall explain, what I think Radhakrishnan may have meant, and I hold to be the case, is that reason or inference forms a part of the process, but it is not involved in the act of insight in which the process culminates.

Obviously, the process under consideration involves the relation of memories to present experiences. However, it is clear from the aforementioned statements, which Radhakrishnan made, that the process is not like the passive Humean account of experience in which the simple relating of past and present experiences creates a habit of expectation.[16] One statement which Radhakrishnan made is to the effect that when one is engaged in this process, he is not an impartial spectator.[17] Another statement, which he made, makes clear that observation is among the powers of the mind which are at work in the process.[18] I think that the foregoing statements, considered together with what has been said about the relation of memories to present experiences, suggests that present impressions and particular related memories are brought together in what Martin Heidegger would call a particular directed focus of concern.

Based upon what has been said, so far, I think that integral insight can be partially described as a directed or intentional process of awareness in which particular memories and present impressions are brought to bear upon a certain focus · of concern or attention.

It seems clear to me that the integral process, as described above, is based on one's experience and reasoning about that experience; it is not simply an emotional response to experience or some fanciful thought.

As I mentioned earlier, Radhakrishnan sometimes spoke as if inference were a part of integral insight.[19] On the face of it, such a view is inconsistent with his statement that integral insight is a non-inferential process.[20] However, given the foregoing difference between the integral process and the integral insight in which the process culminates, it seems logically consistent and coherent that inference forms a part of the past experiences which are brought to bear on a particular focus of concern. To be more specific, reasoning would have taken place with the study of a subject, reflection upon that study, etc. However, the act of insight, which arises after present impressions are brought together with past related memories regarding a particular focus of concern, does not involve reason or inference. This act is such that one gains insight into a problem, situation, condition, or aspect of life. An insight might be in the form of a hunch, an inspiration, an inkling, or what Martin Heidegger might have called an "opening" to Being. I shall discuss Heidegger's views on openness or receptivity in Chapter III.

Based on Radhakrishnan's descriptions of integral insight, my own thinking on the subject, and Heidegger's notion of a focus of concern, I depict intuition or integral insight as a directed or intentional process of the mind which culminates in an act of insight. Unlike Radhakrishnan, I hold that intuition, as I have described it, is *not* a non-discursive form of knowledge. Neither is it an independent way of gaining knowledge, because, as I have explained, it is only one means to knowledge.

Actually, I take intuition to be one of four primary means to knowledge which are interrelated. The four means are: sense perception, intuition, reason and revelation. Via sense experience, one becomes aware of the physical or material aspects of experience. Via mundane uses of intuition, one becomes aware of those aspects of experience which either unify[21] or transcend that which is perceived by the senses. Via reason, one structures what is sensibly perceived or intuited. Also, it is reason which enables one to construct and also to analyze the reasoning process whereby one determines if an inference from premises to a conclusion, i.e., a belief, is warranted. Finally, there is revelation. Although, there are different views as to the nature of revelation, it is Heidegger's view which makes a great deal of sense in regard to human understanding, and which I draw on to explain both that understanding and the transcendent experience in Chapter V.

Given that intuition is an integral process of the mind which culminates in an act of insight, and assuming that it is one means to knowledge, I want to consider two kinds of intuition which I have identified, namely, penetrative and creative. First I will make clear what I take to be the two kinds of intuition, or integral insight, and then I will consider what Radhakrishnan took to be six different types of intuition. I suggest that, with one exception, what he calls "types" of intuition, are simply different expressions of what I take to be the two kinds of intuition. The exception which I will discuss is, in my view, not a kind of intuition or an expression thereof. Turning now to my account of the two kinds of intuition which I have identified, they are as follows:

Penetrative Insight

On a mundane level, penetrative insight is an insight into the structure of a problem, a situation or condition; and, as I shall explain in Chapter V, at a transmundane level, it is an insight into the threshold of what Martin Heidegger calls "Revealed Being."

Focusing on the mundane level of penetrative insight, again, it is the insight into the structure of a problem, or a situation or condition. I think that the structures which one recognizes vary from the simple to the complex.

Penetrative insights into simple structures having to do with problems include when one suddenly "sees":

   (a) a better way to perform a task.

   (b) how to go about learning some subject, language, instrument, sport, or activity.

   (c) how to more effectively organize or reorganize some material.

(d) how to be more productive.

(e) how to handle one's time more efficiently.

(f) how to put together the parts to form some object.

(g) how to repair some broken object, or mend some torn object.

(h) how to redo something, so that it operates more efficiently, e.g., rewiring an old house such that, beyond codes, the wiring meets the future needs of the owners.

(i) how to more efficiently handle one's money.

This list could go on and on, but the point is that there are times, when one focuses on some new challenge, or some way of doing something that one has done, and suddenly thinks "Ah ha! I see." These insights are quite common for one who has developed and trusts her or his intuition.

Penetrative insight into simple structures having to do with situations or conditions include:

(a) when one finds oneself with a group of strangers at a social gathering, and one is instinctively drawn to a person(s) sans any verbal or body language.

(b) on a job interview, when one instinctively feels that she/he does not belong at that particular business or institution, etc.

(c) meeting someone for the first time, and sans verbal or body language, one picks up bad or good "vibes."

(d) Seeing or meeting someone, and somehow "knowing" that you two will be friends.

(e) recognizing a "soul mate" or significant other upon first encounter.

(f) "sensing" potential danger in a situation before any physical or verbal signs have been given.[22]

(g) in a social situation, "knowing" when you do not belong in a particular place, or with particular people, sans physical, or verbal clues. (In this situation, one has a distinct feeling of discomfort.)

(h) suddenly recognizing the unspoken hierarchy or tensions that exist in a group.

There are penetrative insights into either problems or situations which involve more complex structures. These structures are not different in kind than the simple structures, they are just more complex, and often less pertinent information is available. Some examples of this kind of insight are:

(a) a physician who is able to cure a rare disease because of a hunch as to its nature, and a hunch as to the required treatment.

(b) a nurse, who seeing a patient in the emergency ward is able to "see" what the attending physician had not seen, namely, the condition from which the patient is suffering, and, thereby, save the patient's life. (This happened to one of my students who is a nurse.)[23]

(c) one who can "see" unusual trends or patterns forming in the financial market or with particular financial situations.

(d) "knowing," when and where to take a chance in business – whether it has to do with investments, a new undertaking, or a radical change to an existing organization – when that "knowing" is not simply the result of established data or research, etc. (This is the kind of insight which successful entrepreneurs have.)

(e) one who has developed a sense of timing as to when and where to act.

(f) one who can "see" in a timely fashion, when a particular change in focus, orientation or goal is required.

(g) one who can "see" what is needed at a given time for her or his self-development.

(h) a holistic awareness of one's state of health, involving emotional and mental, as well as physical states of well being.

As I have indicated, besides the mundane uses of penetrative insight, described above, there are penetrative insights into Being, or more specifically, the threshold of what Heidegger calls "Revealed Being." This use of penetrative insight will be discussed at length in Chapter V, so suffice it to say, in this context, that this use of insight together with

Revealed Being, form transcendence or transcendent awareness. Also, as I shall explain, this kind of insight seems to
require both a disciplined and meditative way of life.

Creative Insight

There are two forms of creative insight, which I have
identified, and will herewith only briefly describe, as I devote
Chapter IV to a consideration of the use of intuition, i.e.,
creative insight, in creativity:

One form of creative insight is an insight into a chain of
links or transitions which can lead to the solution of a problem,
or an explanation of the links. This is the kind of insight
which is used in mathematics and logic.[24]

Regarding mathematics, in Chapter IV, I will examine what
the two eminent thinkers, whom I mentioned earlier, namely,
Jules Henri Poincaré (a world renowned mathematician) and
Michael Polanyi (a great thinker who was both a scientist and
a philosopher), have said about the use of intuition in
mathematics. As I will make clear when I discuss their views
on the subject, I take the kind of intuition which they consider
to be what I am calling "creative insight."

Regarding logic, Radhakrishnan had something to say about
the use of intuition in logic. In fact, he took logic to be one
of the types of intuition. I will consider what he said about
logic shortly.

Let us turn now to another form of creative insight, namely,
an insight into a series of events which may lead to an
eventuality. This is the kind of insight which is generally
associated with acts of creativity, although, as I have indicated
above, and will explain in Chapter IV, creativity in mathematics
(or logic) seems to involve the first form of creative insight
which I have described. Creative insight, in this second form
being considered, namely, an insight into a series of events
which may lead to an eventuality, is involved when one has
an insight into a happening or happenings in the changing
world, or the fluid ideas about aspects of the changing world.
These insights can and do take place in most fields of endeavor,

e.g., art, architecture, poetry, philosophy, physics, biology, astronomy, medicine, literature, cultural anthropology, etc. not to mention the insight of inventors of all kinds.

I will consider both the nature of creativity, and the use of the foregoing forms of creative insight in creativity, in Chapter IV.

Having set forth my own theory of the two kinds of intuition, or integral insight, let me now briefly consider what Radhakrishnan took to be six types of intuition.[25] As I indicated earlier, with one exception, I take what Radhakrishnan identified as six types of intuition, or integral insight, to be simply various expressions or uses of the kinds of intuition, which I have identified, in different areas of thought or experience. After a brief description of each of the types, I shall explain which kind of intuition, namely, penetrative or creative, that I think applies.

To the best of my knowledge, Radhakrishnan did not offer a systematic description of these types.[26] However, following is a list of the types, with some comments by Radhakrishnan, and/or Robert Browning, a scholar who wrote about the types of intuition in Radhakrishnan's philosophy,[27] and some of my responses:

Logical

With regard to logical insight, Radhakrishnan said: "In every logical proof, there is a grasping of the intellectual togetherness as a whole, an intuition of the whole as sustained by the different steps."[28] In the foregoing passage, Radhakrishnan seemed to imply that one can have a hunch about what can be proven, and the steps involved in a proof. Of course, the hunch can only be proven or disproven by a step by step reasoning process.

I think that what I have identified as one kind of creative insight, namely, the insight into a chain of steps leading to the solution of a problem can be applied here.

Scientific

In *An Idealist View of Life,* Radhakrishnan said that the creative work in science is a synthetic insight which advances by leaps. He adds that a new truth altogether unknown comes into being suddenly and spontaneously owing to the intense and concentrated interest in the problem.[29]

It does seem clear from what Radhakrishnan said that scientific discovery involves the form of creative insight which I have described as an insight into a series of events which may lead to some eventuality. To further this view, I will consider Polanyi's thoughts on the use of intuition in scientific discovery in Chapter IV.

Aesthetic

According to Radhakrishnan, an aesthetic creation is not just the result of an artist's inspiration, or that which evokes a response from an observer. He held that an aesthetic creation conveys religious and/or moral truths. This view is in keeping with traditional Hindu views of art. Radhakrishnan also seems to have held that a person's aesthetic sensitivity, i.e., what she or he intuits, is dependent not only on her or his experience, but upon the level of one's self-development.[30] This view is consistent with the Hindu views of the karmic law which I have described in Chapter I.

I suggest that the kind of insight which is employed in aesthetic appreciation is what I call "penetrative insight." However, the artist's creation would, according to my theory, involve both penetrative and creative insights. In Chapter III, I will briefly present Heidegger's views on the use of intuition in artistic creations.

Moral Insight

According to Robert Browning, Radhakrishnan held that man intuits moral principles.[31] Furthermore, according to Browning, Radhakrishnan seems to have held that the clearness or correctness of such intuitions depends on one's ethical sensitivity. Again, this view is consistent with the Hindu belief that one's moral development would reflect her or his level of karmic development. Also, as I noted in an article involving the thought of Radhakrishnan on intuition, Radhakrishnan held to the fundamental notions of yoga development which I introduced in Chapter I, and will explain in more depth in Chapter V.[32] According to this view, before one can have spiritual insight, she or he must still the mind, which involves stages of what we in the West call "meditation." In turn, in order to still the mind, one must have mastered moral restraints such as non-harm, etc.

My own view regarding the case of integral insight into moral issues is that one can have insights which affect moral decisions, but moral action is the result of character development and education, not insight. However, I do agree with Radhakrishnan, and the ancient Yoga School of Philosophy, that moral development is necessary for what Radhakrishnan calls "spiritual insight." I will mention this spiritual insight shortly.

Philosophical Thought

To my knowledge, Radhakrishnan did not explain what he meant by philosophical intuition. However, Browning considered a type of intuition which might be regarded as philosophical in that it gives insight into the scheme of things entire. Furthermore, even though Browning expressed some uncertainty as to whether or not Radhakrishnan would have accepted this category of intuition,[33] I suggest that the following description of this category may be what Radhakrishnan had in mind when he spoke of philosophical insight.

Browning called the type of intuition, mentioned above, "Descrying of Complex Structures of Fact and Possible Fact."[34] The account of this type of intuition is lengthy and somewhat obscure. However, in the account, Browning describes the bounds or limits of a structure as the whole of a situation, a field of study, a game, etc.[35] Based on what Browning said, the structure would appear to be the whole of a focus of attention or area of concentration. Browning says that there is a range of the kinds of structures from a specific structure to a vague metaphysical framework.[36]

In my view, what Browning has described above is similar to what I have identified as penetrative insight. However, in retrospect, I believe that Browning's account of insight into a structure undoubtedly affected my formative views of penetrative insight.[37] As I explained earlier, I hold that penetrative insight is used both at the mundane and the transmundane level. At a mundane level, penetrative insight is an insight into either the structure of some problem or a situation or condition. Transmundane insight is mentioned in the following section.

Spiritual Insight

Radhakrishnan's view of ultimate reality is Hindu, and complex. In Chapter V, I discuss one aspect of what I take to be his view,[38] namely, the Advaita Vedānta view that reality is unified . However, for the purposes at hand, suffice it to say that for Radhakrishnan, spiritual intuition, or integral insight, meant that one realizes the unity of reality.

My views of spiritual insight differ from Radhakrishnan's. As I have indicated earlier, I take this insight to be penetrative. Also, as I have mentioned, this kind of insight will be considered in depth in Chapter V.

In Chapter V, I consider what some persons have referred to as the "mystical experience" or "spiritual experience," and I call "transcendence" or "transcendent awareness."

What I try to show is that transcendence is comprised of penetrative insight into the threshold of what Heidegger called "Revealed Being."

The Development and Uses of Intuition

Before leaving the subject of what I take to be the nature and uses of intuition, I need to take due account of the fact that intuition, as well as intelligence, has to be developed, if it is to be used effectively. Leaving aside, for the moment, the question of the nature of intuition, there is also the question of the development of it, so that it can be used. Hindus, who, in general, believe in intuition, have developed the ability to use it. Their response to someone who would deny its use might well be. "How do you know? You have not developed the ability to use it!"

What happens, I believe, with regard to uses of intuition, is that one will have an insight, but quickly "shut it off," as it were, because of a distrust of the insight. What is needed, is that one develop her or his insight along with her or his reasoning skills. Of course part of the development involves a certain freedom of thought whereby after subjecting an insight to reason, one acts on the insight. When one does this, she or he does not act irrationally or unreasonably. What is gained is a broader and deeper understanding of one's life experiences, and perhaps some insight into reality itself.

The foregoing view which I have offered is in keeping with the right-brain/left-brain theory. Basically, according to this theory, the functions of the left side of the brain involve analysis, computation, reason, etc., while the right side of the brain which takes in the larger "picture," or view of experience, involves intuition.[39] If one accepts this theory, it seems obvious that many persons, especially in the Western traditions, have developed the left brain, with disregard to the right.

In my view, we need to use all of our mental capacities, including both the reasoning skills and intuition, if we are to live full, rich, meaningful lives. As one who has taught formal and informal logic, and epistemology, I recognize the importance of using the tools of reason. However, as a person working not only to explain, but to develop, intuitive powers, as well as reasoning powers, I know that intuition is indeed "the cutting edge of the mind's life."

SUMMARY

I have presented my view as to the nature of intuition, or integral insight. I culled the core idea of this view from Radhakrishnan. However, at times he spoke as if reason were a part of integral insight, and at times he spoke as if integral insight did not involve reason. Based on his descriptions of the process involved, some of my own thought, and Martin Heidegger's notion of a focus of concern, I determined that intuition is an intentional process of the mind, which culminates in an act of insight. The process is one in which present impressions are brought together with past related memories on a focus of concern. The process involves reason, in that reason was used to form a number of the memories, and perhaps also in the relating of past memories to present impressions. However, the act of insight in which the process culminates, does not involve reason. It is that "cutting edge of the mind's life. It can be described as: a hunch, an inkling, a "seeing into" or "taking in," or as Heidegger might say, an "openness."[40] In common vernacular, it is the "Ah Ha! I see!"

Unlike Radhakrishnan, I do not take intuition to be a form of knowledge, or a non-discursive way of gaining knowledge, for as I have explained in Chapter I, knowledge is by its nature discursive. I do, however, take intuition to be one means to knowledge which is complementary to reason, and can be checked by reason.

Another major difference between Radhakrishnan's views of intuition, or integral insight, and mine, is that I have identified two basic kinds of intuition. As I have explained, I think that all but one of what Radhakrishnan identified as six types of intuition are really only expressions of the use of intuition in different areas of thought or experience. Furthermore, I have suggested that the kinds of intuition which I have identified explain five of the six types of intuition which he mentions. There is one type, namely moral, which I do not accept as a kind of insight.

Reiterating the nature of the two kinds of intuition which I have described in this chapter, they are:

Penetrative
   (a)   an insight into the structure of a problem or a situation or condition which ranges from the simple to the complex

(b) an insight into the threshold of what Heidegger called "Revealed Being," thereby forming transcendent awareness (I will discuss this kind of insight in Chapter V.)

Creative

(a) an insight into a chain of links or transitions which lead to the solution of a problem or an explanation of the links.

(b) an insight into a series of events that can lead to some eventuality.

As I explained in the preface of the book, without a recognition of intuition, which is a natural part of the "mind's life," some experiences are difficult to explain, and others are impossible. Given the two kinds of insight, penetrative and creative, which I have identified, one can account for the following kinds of experiences: (1) having a "calling" to a particular profession, can be explained by penetrative insight (a), and, also, depending on the nature of one's profession, creative insight may also be involved (b); (2) the solving of a murder mystery, which I analyze in Chapter III, would seem to involve both penetrative and creative insight (penetrative a and creative b); (3) Certain scientific discoveries, which I will consider in Chapter IV, can be explained by creative insight (b); (4) certain mathematical discoveries and solutions to problems, can be explained by creative insight (a); and (5) acts of genius, which I discuss in Chapter IV, are explained by an appeal to creative insight (a and b). Finally, the possibility of those experiences, that are sometimes referred to as "spiritual" or "mystical," which cannot be explained without an appeal to penetrative intuition (b) and/ or revelation, are made clear in the analysis of transcendence which I undertake in Chapter V. I end this chapter with a brief explanation of the need to develop intuitive powers.

ENDNOTES

1. Sarvepalli Radhakrishnan's core idea of intuition also played a role in my Doctoral Dissertation, *Intuition as an Integral Process of the*

Mind, wherein I compare the views of Radhakrishnan and Martin Heidegger regarding the subject of intuition.

2.   As I explain in Chapter IV, on occasion, Michael Polany did use the term "creative insight," however, what he meant by "creative insight," is not what I mean by the term, although his description of the process involved supports my view.

3.   Sarvepalli Radhakrishnan, "Reply to Critics," in *The Philosophy of Sarvepalli Radhakrishnan*, ed. by Paul Arthur Schilpp. p. 791.

4.   *Ibid.*

5.   *Ibid.*

6.   *Ibid.*, p. 792.

7.   *Ibid.*, pp. 790–791.

8.   *Ibid.*, p. 792.

9.   *Contemporary Indian Philosophy*, ed. by Sarvepalli Radhakrishnan and J. H. Muirhead, pp. 486–487.

10. Radhakrishnan, "Reply to Critics," pp. 790–791.

11. *Ibid.*; and *Contemporary Indian Philosophy*, pp. 486–487.

12. *Contemporary Indian Philosophy*, pp. 486–487.

13. Radhakrishnan, "Reply to Critics," pp. 790–791.

14. *Ibid.*, p. 792.

15. *Ibid.*, p. 791.

16. *Ibid.*, p. 792.

17. *Ibid.*

18. *Ibid.*

19. *Ibid.*

20. *Ibid.*, p. 791; and *Radhakrishnan*, ed. by Robert A. McDermott, p. 153.

21. By "unify," I mean bring together, as in the case of the detective who can "see" the series of events leading to a crime, based on certain information, plus intuition (I shall discuss this in Chapter III).

22. According to his fellow officers and friends, my father, who was a Commander in the U.S. Navy, and a Captain in the Maritime Service, could be anywhere in the world, often at some bar, when he would tell his friends that they should all leave, as trouble was brewing. No one else saw or heard anything, but, apparently my father could intuit the danger, as indeed some brawl or something worse would subsequently occur.

23. The student Cheryl Ajemian, R.N., C.E.N., was working in the emergency room, when a young and healthy looking female patient

came in complaining about just not feeling right. There were no discernable signs or symptoms of acute distress. Hence, the patient was determined to be non-acute. (The testing did not include a chest auscultation, as that is done only for a pulmonary or cardiac case.) However, while the patient was being checked for vital signs and being interviewed by a co-worker, for some unknown reason to Cheryl, she put a stethoscope to the patient's chest. She heard no heart sounds. She knew instantly that the patient was in cardiac temponade, and immediately rushed to find a physician on duty. When the physician found no heart sounds, a cardiologist was found. After treatment, the patient recovered. Cheryl said that even though the cardiologist praised her for a "good call," and she considers herself to be an excellent emergency nurse, there were no symptoms for the condition, yet something made her vary the usual procedure, and thereby save a patient's life.

24. It is not at all uncommon for a mathematician or logician, or even someone who often does proofs, such as a teacher, to have an insight into either the transitions to a conclusion, or even the conclusion. However, the insight or hunch can only be proven or disproven by the step by step reasoning process.

25. Radhakrishna, "Reply to Critics," p. 791.

26. Radhakrishnan did consider aspects of some of the types of intuition, i.e., expressions of integral insight, in his work *An Idealist View of Life*, pp. 127–174.

27. Robert W. Browning, "Reason and Types of Intuition in Radhakrishnan's Philosophy" in *The Philosophy of Sarvepalli Radhakrishnan*, ed. by Paul Arthur Schilpp, pp. 173–277.

28. *Ibid.*, p. 189.

29. Radhakrishnan, *An Idealist View of Life*, p. 175.

30. Browning, "Reason and Types of Intuition in Radhakrishnan's Philosophy," pp. 207–212.

31. *Ibid.*, pp. 198–200.

32. Hope Fitz, "The Nature and Significance of Intuition in Patañjali's Yoga Sūtra and in the Philosophical Writings of Radhakrishnan," published in *The Journal of Religious Studies*, Patiala [Punjab], India, Punjabi University, Vol. XXVI, Spring–Autumn 1995, Nos. 1 & 2, pp. 9–21.

33. Browning, "Reason and Types of Intuition in Radhakrishnan's Philosophy," p. 181.

34. *Ibid.*, p. 181.

35. *Ibid.*, p. 189.

36. *Ibid.*, 187.

37. As I was recently reviewing the material on Browning's account of insight into structure, it struck me that his account had affected my formative thoughts about penetrative insight.

38. Radhakrishnan, "Reply to Critics," p. 796. Radhakrishnan, as well as Gandhi, held that there is a personal or active aspect as well as an impersonal aspect to ultimate reality.

39. Jacquelyn Wonder and Priscilla Donovan, *Whole Brain Thinking*, Chapter I.

40. As we shall see in Chapter III, Heidegger spoke of human receptivity to what was revealed in experience as an "openness."

CHAPTER III

INTUITION AS A MEANS
TO KNOWLEDGE

In the previous chapter, I have analyzed and described intuition, i.e., integral insight, as a process of the mind which is grounded in reason, but culminates in an act of insight which does not involve reason. Furthermore, I have identified two types of intuition or insight, namely, penetrative and creative. Based upon what I have said thus far about intuition, I think it is evident that it is a natural function of the mind which is necessary for human experience and an understanding of experience. Also, I believe I have made clear that although the process of intuition is natural to human thought, it has to be developed. In this respect, it is similar to intelligence. This development, as I indicated earlier, requires a certain freedom of thought, effort, and discipline.

In addition to what I have said above, I have argued that intuition is not itself a form of knowledge, nor an independent way of gaining knowledge. Instead, I take intuition to be one of four primary interrelated means to knowledge. Again, the means to knowledge are: sense perception, intuition, reason, and revelation. Via sense perception, one becomes aware of the sensible or material aspects of what Heidegger would describe as what is presented or revealed in experience. Via intuition, one becomes aware of those aspects of what is presented which are not sensible.[1] Via reason, one structures what is sensibly perceived or intuited. Also, it is reason which enables one to construct and also to analyze logical arguments, i.e., to determine if an inference from premises to a conclusion is warranted. Regarding revelation there are various views as to what it is, several of which I will discuss in the last chapter of the book. However, it is Martin Heidegger's view which I find meaningful, and appeal to in order to explain understanding and transcendence.

In this chapter, I will assume that one is familiar with what I have said about the nature of intuition, and aware that I take it to be one means to knowledge. However, as I explained earlier, because the nature of intuition has been misunderstood (It has been taken to be a non-discursive form or independent way of gaining knowledge.), many rigorous thinkers have not recognized or accepted it as a means to knowledge. This is significant, because the means to knowledge establish the criteria for justification of a belief, and, of course, any critical thinker is concerned that she or he be able to justify a belief. However, until and unless critical thinkers recognize and accept intuition as one means to knowledge, and, thus, as a criterion for justification of a belief, much of human experience is either inadequately explained or is inexplicable.

Based on what I have said above, I want to : (1) consider certain influential philosophies which have either rejected or ignored intuition as a means to knowledge, and make clear how these philosophies have unnecessarily limited human knowledge, (2) explore the criteria for justification of a belief, and (3) show that intuition is a means to knowledge for certain beliefs, and thus, it can and should be accepted as justification for such beliefs. Furthermore, if the criteria for justification of a belief are expanded to include intuition, one can account for much of reality and human experience that is either inadequately explained or is inexplicable without it.

Certain Influential Philosophies in which Intuition is either Rejected or Ignored

In the light of what I have said about the epistemological thrust of the modern and recent periods of philosophy, and traditional views of intuition not being acceptable to rigorous thinkers, it is not surprising that philosophers and other thinkers have rejected or ignored a consideration of intuition.

Two famous modern philosophers who rejected intuition, in their epistemological accounts, were David Hume (1711–1776) and Immanuel Kant (1724–1804). What is clear about Hume's and Kant's philosophies is that since the content of experience is sensible only, perception does not include intuition. Of course, the result of their rejection of intuition, was a limited view of what can be known.

Given Hume's empiricism and theory of ideas, knowledge of the material world is probable at best, and metaphysical and spiritual beliefs are not knowable,[2] hence meaningless.

Kant, although not an empiricist, certainly accepted Hume's belief that what is given in experience is sensible.[3] Kant referred to this given as "the manifold of the given." He also spoke of the perception of the given as "sensible intuition." However, what Kant meant by "sensible intuition" is the taking in of the sensible content of experience. According to Kant's theory of knowledge, in which the Principle of the Understanding, as form,[4] gives structure to or structures the sensible content of experience, there is a necessity to human knowledge which Hume did not recognize.[5] However, the result is a dichotomy between knowledge as appearance, and what something is in and of itself (the *Dinge an Sich*). In my view, in order to gain a degree of necessity regarding human knowledge of the world, Kant locked humans into a realm of appearance. Also, whereas Hume took metaphysics and spiritual thought to be meaningless, Kant, himself a religious man, was forced into viewing such thought as merely speculative.

In either of the philosophies in question, ontology, as the study of Being, was ruled out. I will return to this subject shortly, when I consider Martin Heidegger's criticism of Kant's mind-dependent epistemology, and those philosophies leading to Kant's philosophy, which rule out any serious consideration of Being.

Hume's and Kant's views about the limits of knowledge have influenced much of contemporary philosophy including those writers, whom I mentioned in Chapter I, namely those who are loosely labeled "post modern," post structural," or "deconstructionist." However, as I noted earlier, these writers reject structure in language, which most of them take to be the basis and set the boundaries of knowledge.[6] Generally speaking, they hold that language itself is not based on any set meanings of symbols or signs. Given these views, they conclude that any episteme, i.e., body of knowledge, is constructed, and is not the result of discovering some structure. As I mentioned in Chapter I, some of these thinkers are skeptics with regard to the knowing process, hence, knowledge.[7]

What I think is missing in much of the post modern account of knowledge, is intuition, as I have described it, namely, one means to knowledge.[8] I submit that intuition as one means to knowledge can break through the linguistic boundaries of knowledge. To be more specific, via intuition, as I have described it, one can gain insight into human experience which is not grounded in symbols or signs, etc.

Having briefly touched upon two modern philosophers who rejected intuition as a means to knowledge, and one contemporary philosophical group of thinkers who have in general ignored intuition as a means to knowledge, and pointed out the limitations of knowledge set by such theories, let me now explore the criteria for justification of a belief, and the argument that since intuition is a means to knowledge, it should be accepted as one criterion for justification of a belief.

The Criteria for Justification of a Belief

It seems to me that in examining the criteria for the justification of a belief, one needs to focus on what counts as justification. When one is considering beliefs about experience, I think that the notion of justification which is significant is that which is connoted when one speaks of "justifying" a conclusion of an informal inductive logical argument. When one speaks of "justifying" or "justification" in this sense, one is asking for reasons to support the inference to the conclusion, and to show that those reasons are good and sufficient. Good reasons include those that are true or factual or reasonable to accept, and relevant. In seeking evidence for a reason, one can appeal to authority, statistics, testimony, analogy, a generally accepted body of knowledge which is prevalent in a culture, one's own experience, or to a theory which best explains a given body of data or experience.

Focusing more closely on what will count as justification, it is crucial to note that justification is a broad notion, and that what is required to justify a particular conclusion, or belief, may depend on the nature of that belief. Again, the reasons for a belief are said to justify that belief, and thus warrant an inference to that belief, i.e., conclusion, if the reasons are good and sufficient. Also, there can be no fallacies in the reasoning process.

Concerning the question of what constitutes "good reasons," one must consider the bearing which the reasons have on the belief, and what kind of evidence is available for the reasons. Let us consider a few examples of arguments in which the belief is warranted because the reasons justify the inference to the conclusion.

One of the examples alluded to above could be a claim about the physical world. Perhaps I say that the tides of the ocean are caused by variations in the position of the moon. What I need to give as reasons for my claim are evidential statements that there is indeed a correlation between the variations in the time and place of high water and the variations in the position of the moon, or acknowledgement that this is the accepted theory of the causes of the tides, etc.

The kind of evidence which I am giving as justification for my claim is objectively verifiable, at least in principle. Until the last twenty years or so, what a modern scientist, or philosopher of science, would generally mean by "objectively verifiable" was that what was given in evidence, for a scientific claim or explanation, was both objective and confirmable.[9] However, another standard which does not require confirmability, is what is expressed in a theory called "Inference to the Best Explanation."[10] According to this theory, whatever hypothesis most adequately explains the evidence is the hypothesis which is then accepted.[11] Given this theory, one's belief would have to be in accord with the hypothesis which best explained the evidence, and the evidence would still rest on a standard of objectivity.

Underlying the criterion of objectivity is the standard of public observability. Such is the case because a key meaning of "objective" is: an object perceived or thought which is external to the mind, or real, as opposed to that which is merely subjective, i.e., merely a mental representation.[12] The thinking here is: How could one know that an object which someone claimed to perceive were real, if it were not in principle observable by anyone?

It is significant to note that whereas there has been a shift from 'confirmability to "inference to the best explanation" it is still the case that scientific evidence is, at least in principle, observable. Of course "observable" may range from directly observable to simply traceable or measurable by sophisticated technology or experiments.

Having examined an example of justification for a belief which required objective verifiability, let me turn to several beliefs which I argue involve intuition as a means to knowledge. If intuition is a means to knowledge, then it should be accepted as a criterion for justification of a belief. If one does accept intuition as a criterion for justification of the beliefs which I will consider, and also accepts whatever other reasons are given for each belief, then I think that one can conclude that these beliefs are justified.

The first belief which I want to consider is one concerning who perpetrated a crime and why. Consider a woman detective, "Ms. Sherlock," who has been hired to solve a case of murder. She has come to a decision as to who committed the crime and why. In order to appreciate how she came to this conclusion, let us reflect on the mental processes involved in solving the crime. Imagine, if you will, Ms. Sherlock standing at the scene of the crime (where nothing has been altered, except that the body has been removed, and an outline of the body is now on the floor). There are clues in the room which our lady detective will notice. These clues will have to be "interwoven" with pertinent factual data about the deceased party, suspects, and a motive, etc. Now, what enables a good detective to put the pieces of the puzzle together, and thereby solve a case, is not only reasoning, both inductive and deductive,[13] but intuition. It is intuition, i.e., new hunches and insights, based on the detective's experience, intelligence, character, and intuitive powers, which enable her to distinguish what is relevant or significant in the case, to realize which persons are trustworthy, and to visualize how the crime could have been committed. Note that the first two uses of intuition are penetrative in that the detective sees into the structure of the problem to be solved. The third use of intuition could be explained as partly penetrative, and partly creative, as the detective has to be able to envision the series of events leading to the murder.

As I explained in Chapter II, the penetrative insights, which I described in the foregoing example, are not uncommon. Also, as I explained in Chapter II, when one has such insights, it is really a breakthrough based on: the culmination of one's past experience, including one's reasoning, feeling, other insights, and one's receptivity, etc. Thus, in effect, the insight can be viewed as the "cutting edge of the mind's life," in that the mind in process gathers together and assimilates what it has "taken in," and then when needed, it can "open up" or "reach out" for new pertinent information or the solution to a problem, etc. However, let me reiterate that new areas of insight are based on or grounded in one's past experience, receptivity, etc.

With regard to creative insight, which is also involved in the foregoing example, I believe it is clear from what I said in Chapter II, that this kind of insight is, in general, somewhat rarer than penetrative insight (at least the mundane use of penetrative insight). However, as I indicated earlier, I believe that this is the case because humans need to learn and be encouraged to develop their creative abilities. Again, in the case of the detective, it is the creative insight which can enable her to see or envision the series of events which led to the murder. Note that the information sought is rarely gained by recognition and/or reconstruction alone, because usually, in such cases, many of the "pieces" of the puzzle are missing. However, given the conditions which I mentioned earlier concerning life experience, and the development of intuitive powers, etc., one can become adept at intuiting the missing links in a certain series of steps which lead to a solution.

A second example of a belief for which experience, gained by intuition, can and should be included as justification for the belief, would be that of an inventor who had the foresight to see some product which others did not see. Perhaps both penetrative and creative insight would give the inventor the vision of what she or he would later create, i.e., bring into being, and of course creative insight would be involved in the production of the product.

A third example of a belief for which intuition can and should be accepted as a criterion for justification, is a metaphysical belief, involving penetrative as well as creative insight, which seems to explain some aspect of reality or experience to a number of thinkers. I have in mind a belief of William Blake the great (1757-1827) poet and artist, whose poetry rested on a dialectical metaphysics.[14] Blake held that a natural dialectical tension exists between contraries such as imagination and reason. I will not try to explain Blake's metaphysics which led to this belief, since that is a study unto itself.[15] I will note, however, that Blake's metaphysics seemed to reflect the kind of tension of opposites which is suggested in the metaphysics of Heraclitus.[16] It seems clear to me that Blake was someone who had great penetrative insight into the nature of reality as well as the ability to express his insight in poetry, and the paintings, and engravings which accompany his poetry.[17] Given my account of intuition, the expressions of this ability would be the result of creative insight.

The reasons given for the foregoing beliefs having to do with intuition, would not, nor could they be confined to a justification based on objective verifiability. I say this because, given what I have said about the subject, I think it is clear that a requirement of objective verifiability is that the content of experience is sensible. Hence objective verifiability would limit one's beliefs to those of the physical world or the world of nature. Such is the case because evidence is available which would meet the standard of objective verifiability. This evidence is based on sense experience and reason, and it is observable, in principle. One can either confirm that evidence or give a theory of explanation for it which is supported by testing.

Since I mentioned William Blake, who was first and foremost a poet, I think that it is worth mentioning that Martin Heidegger would regard what I have identified as penetrative insight, as well as creative insight, to be primarily the gift of the poet.[18] He held that creative persons, especially certain poets,[19] are able to reveal truth or reality to others in their creative expressions.[20] Of course, the revelations of truth presuppose insights and expressions thereof, so the poets in question are those rare human beings who have both breadth and depth of knowledge, and insight into the nature and meaning of life.[21]

I appreciate Heidegger's view of the poet's insight. However, I do not believe that poets are any more gifted in this area than other creative thinkers such as certain philosophers, artists, scientists, psychologists, etc. Heidegger, himself, had such a span of insight. With regard to Heidegger's insight, let me conclude this chapter with a brief sketch of his ontology. This account of Being involves intuition or what Heidegger might call an "openness" or receptivity to Being. Furthermore, it is justifiable albeit not objectively so.

First, it is important to note that Heidegger was a phenomenologist, and as such he accepted the fundamental idea of phenomenology, namely, that what is given in experience, i.e., phenomena, is not limited to sense experience. In fact, some phenomenologists, following the thinking of Edmond Husserl, held that questions such as existence should be suspended. This suspension, called an epoché is similar to René Descarte's notion of Cartesian Doubt, i.e., holding some judgment in abeyance. The difference, of course, is that with Descartes, certain beliefs were suspended until a firm foundation of knowledge could be established for the beliefs. In the case of Husserl's epoché, the question of existence was simply bracketed, so that dreams, wishes, feelings, aspirations, etc. could be included in what was called "phenomena."

Although there is not agreement among phenomenologists as to the phenomenological method *per se*, they do generally agree that there are several steps involved in the method. Basically, I take these steps to be: (1) a careful observation of the content of a particular experience; (2) a reflection on the content of the experience which involves an analysis of that content; (3) a synthesis of that content with one's previous experiences (In my view, the synthesis is not random, but is influenced by what one takes to be meaningful in life);[22] and (4) an understanding of the content of the experience in the light of its meaning.[23]

Rather than phenomena, *per se*, Heidegger was interested in the ontological structure which underlies phenomena. In other words, it was Being which interested him. I shall consider the subject in more detail in Chapter V, but for the present purpose, let us note that Revealed Being, i.e., the Being which is revealed or given (*es gibt*) in experience to Dasein, i.e., human beings who are the only beings capable of understanding Being, is not limited to sense experience.

The belief which I am about to give will become clearer after I examine Heidegger's ontological views in the chapter on transcendence. However, I think that one can consider the reasons for the belief prior to this examination, and, furthermore, these reasons are such that one can both understand and appreciate my claim that the reasons do, indeed, justify the belief.

Objective verifiable evidence is not available for Heidegger's belief that understanding involves a relation between Revealed Being, i.e., that which is given to or revealed to *Dasein*, and

Dasein's awareness of and receptivity to that which is revealed.[24] The reason that objectively verifiable evidence is not available for this belief is because metaphysical questions of ontology, i.e., the nature of Being, or cosmology, i.e., the origin, development and structure of reality, transcend what is purely physical, or known via the senses. Since objective verifiability is not possible with regard to Heidegger's belief, what would justify this belief? Again, in order to warrant an inference to a belief, i.e., a conclusion, of an informal inductive argument, the reasons must be good, and sufficient. Good reasons are those which are true or factual or reasonable to accept, and relevant.

Some of the reasons which Heidegger offered to justify his belief, that I consider reasonable to accept, and relevant are:

1. the need to overcome the historical trend of metaphysics from Aristotle to Kant which has culminated in Kant's subjectivist view of reality that obstructs the search for Being[25] (Given this view, knowledge is the result of the human mind structuring what is sensibly perceived. Furthermore, what can be known is limited to appearance. Since humans cannot know what something is, in itself, aside from appearance, insight into the beliefs about Being, i.e., the nature of reality, and/or God, become purely speculative).

2. a reexamination of the pre-Socratic views of Being or what Heidegger called "the Being of beings."[26] According to Heidegger's research, the early Greeks took *physis*, which is usually translated as natural or physical, to mean the gathering together and bringing forth of Being which could, but need not, be expressed in language. Based on this view, the Being of beings can be described as the emergent, abiding, presence, or that by which all things emerge into presence as to what they are and endure.[27]

3. the realization that there is not Revealed Being without Dasein, i.e., human beings, as the beings who are capable of understanding what is revealed, i.e., given in experience.[28]

4. the realization that what can be known is not limited

to sense experience and reason (Heidegger considered revelation as what is given or presented in experience).[29]

5. based on premises 1–4, human knowledge or understanding of reality is not a constructive enterprise, nor is it
limited to what is perceived via the senses.

6. extensive research into the explication of Being.[30]

7. based on premises 1–6, a theory of explanation according
to which Revealed Being is not an entity, but a happening,
presencing or coming forth of life.[31]

8. Dasein's understanding is based on her or his "openness"
or receptivity to Being.

Given the foregoing reasons, and others which are too
numerous and/or involved to mention here, Heidegger con-
cluded that human understanding involves a relationship
between what is revealed to Dasein, i.e., Revealed Being, and
Dasein's awareness of and receptivity to what is revealed.[32]

What impresses many recent or contemporary critical
thinkers about Heidegger's philosophy, in general, is that
what he says is so carefully researched and rigorously reasoned. Also, in the final analysis, Heidegger's account of
Being, and Dasein's understanding of Being, makes "sense"
of life experience, and it enables one to hold a scientific world
view which is not at odds with the view of a transcendent
reality. I will have more to say about transcendent reality in
Chapter V.

Returning to the question of justification for a belief, again
let me state that since intuition is a means to knowledge, then
it should be accepted as one criterion for justification of a
belief. I think that in the examples of beliefs involving intuition, I have shown that intuition is without question a
means to knowledge, and thus it should be accepted as a
criterion for justification of these beliefs. In my judgment,
I think that these beliefs are clearly justified.

Summing up my arguments in the foregoing consideration
of the criteria for justification of a belief, I have shown that
criteria are not the same for each belief; and since intuition
is indeed a means to knowledge for certain beliefs, the criteria

for justification should be expanded to include intuition. Also, as I have made clear, if the criteria are so expanded, then one can account for many aspects of life that are inexplicable or meaningless without it.

ENDNOTES

1.　These aspects include: what unites sensible data, i.e., a structure, a situation or condition, the chain of transitions leading to a solution or a series of events leading to some eventuality.

2.　Since, for Hume: 1. all ideas have their origins in sensible impressions, 2. the natural associations of ideas are involuntary, and 3. philosophical ideas are based on the natural associations, it is clear that there cannot be metaphysical ideas such as substances, e.g., a self or God, or any explanations of ultimate reality.

3.　As is well known, Kant held that knowledge starts with sensible experience, but it is not determined by experience. Rather, the sensible content of experience is structured by the Principles of the Understanding.

4.　Since the Principles of the Understanding, including space, time, and the categories, structure or forms the sensible content of experience, it is referred to as form.

5.　Also, since cause and effect are included in the categories of the understanding, the argument for causal necessity is strengthened.

6.　The view of the structuralists who were focused on semiology.

7.　As I stated in Chapter I, these thinkers included Michel Foucault and Richard Rorty.

8.　A friend and colleague Robert Christensen, Associate Professor of History, Emeritus, who has done extensive research on this subject for a book in progress, says that he does not think it is correct to claim that all post moderns reject a consideration of intuition. However, I doubt that they view it as a means to knowledge which is complementary to reason. If they did, I think that they would see that intuition is not bound by linguistic barriers. In other words, one can gain insight not grounded in symbols or signs.

9.　According to W. L. Reese, in the *Dictionary of Philosophy and Religion*, under *verifiability*, it was Rudolph Carnap who modified the strict sense of verifiability, according to which concepts must be supported by operational evidence in order to be meaningful, to a notion of testability or confirmability.

10. Gilbert Harmon expands on this view in his book *Thought*, Princeton University Press, New Jersey, c. 1973.

11. *Ibid.*

12. *American Heritage Dictionary.*

13. I mean "inductive" and "deductive" in the logical sense in which conclusions of inductive arguments are only probable, and those from "deductive" arguments are certain.

14. I was privileged to work with Dr. Elizabeth Sewell, the Newton and William Blake scholar, and a poet in her own right, when Mount St. Mary's, Los Angeles, where I was teaching, hired her to teach a course in "Genius and Creativity" with two English professors and me. From Dr. Sewell, and from my own research, I learned to appreciate Blake's genius.

15. What one would need to fully explain the metaphysics, which underlies the poetry, is the symbolic meaning both in the poetry and the pictures which accompany each poem.

16. What I found in my research was that Blake held a dialectical metaphysics, similar to that of Heraclitus, in which there is a tension of opposites that generates change and development.

17. When I was a reader at the Huntington Research Library in San Marino, California, there were a group of scholars who were devoted to Blake research and publication.

18. Martin Heidegger, "The Origin of the Work of Art," in *Poetry, Language, Thought*, p. 73.

19. *Ibid.*

20. *Ibid.*, p. 75.

21. Martin Heidegger, "Remembrance of the Poet," *Existence and Being*, p. 263; "What is Metaphysics," in *Existence and Being*, p. 360; and the "Essence of Poetry," in *Existence and Being*, p. 281; and Hope Fitz, *Intuition as an Integral Process of the Mind*, pp. 88-94.

22. I think that there is a grid or structure of meaning that begins to form when persons are very young. Take two small children to a zoo, and then later question them about what was meaningful for each of them. The answers are quite likely to differ. I think that as humans mature, and have more experiences, the grid of meaning influences what they focus upon, and how they synthesize the content of experience.

23. Given what I have said about the grid of meaning, etc., I think it is clear that understanding the content of experience would be, in large measure, due to what was meaningful.

24. Stephen A. Erickson, *Language and Being*, New Haven and London, Yale University Press, 1970, p. 146. As Stephen Erickson says, "The revelation of an understanding of Being is at the same time the revelation of Being understood, a consequence of the doctrine of intentionality, and the disclosure of Being is simultaneously a disclosure of the understanding-of-being, a consequence of Heidegger's phenomenological development of the epistemological implications of Kant's central acritico-transcendental thesis." See also Martin Heidegger, *Being and Time*, p. 32.

25. Martin Heidegger, "The Limitation of Being," especially pp. 157–172 in *An Introduction to Metaphysics*.

26. Martin Heidegger, *What is Called Thinking?* pp. 235, 238, 244; Martin Heidegger, "What are Poets For?" in *Poetry, Language, and Thought*, pp. 100–102, 132; Martin Heidegger, *The Question of Being*, p. 95.

27. *Ibid.*; Martin Heidegger, *An Introduction to Metaphysics*, pp. 11–14; William J. Richardson, S.F. *Heidegger: Through Phenomenology to thought*, p. 5. In the last two works cited, what is discussed is the early Greek meaning of the term *physis*. According to Heidegger, *physis*, which is usually translated as natural or physical, meant Being to the early Greeks. However, what the early Greeks meant by "Being," is what Heidegger called the "Being of beings," and I sometimes refer to as the "Being-ness of beings."

28. Martin Heidegger, *Being and Time*, p. 255.

29. *Ibid.*, pp. 182–188; Martin Heidegger, *On Time and Being*, pp. 2, 5–8, 10–19.

30. Heidegger was a philologist as well as a philosopher. The more one studies his many works concerned with Being, the more one appreciates his work with early Greek thought, and the "digging" for meanings of relevant terms in Greek and German.

31. Martin Heidegger, *On Time and Being*, pp. 2, 5, 6, 8, 10, 11, 19.

32. Stephen A. Erickson, *Language and Being: An Analytic Phenomenology*, New Haven, Yale University Press, *c.* 1970, p. 146.

CHAPTER IV

THE USE OF INTUITION IN CREATIVITY

In Chapter II, I explained the nature of intuition, described its uses, and argued that it is one means to knowledge. Also, I identified two kinds of intuition, namely, penetrative insight and creative insight. In the examples of the uses of creative insight, I have given some indication as to the role of creative insight in creativity.

In this chapter, I am concerned to consider the nature of creativity and the role of creative insight in creativity. However, before I can undertake my objectives, I must consider what is meant by "creativity."

The key concepts involved in the meaning of "creativity" are: the ability to create; the product of creation; and the originality and value of that product. Traditionally, it was assumed that special talent or genius[1] is necessary to produce new and valuable entities.[2] This production was taken to be the essence of creativity. Nowadays, however, it is rather popular among some professional researchers, as well as nonprofessionals, to insist that the potential for creativity exists in everyone.

Based upon what I have said, there seem to be two fundamental perspectives regarding creativity. According to the first perspective, creativity is a gift of genius or special talent, which certain individuals have. This gift is recognizable by the degree of originality and value of the creation. In the case of the genius, the creations can be described as involving radical change, and being far-reaching in effect and/or value.[3]

According to the second perspective, mentioned above, each person possesses a potential to be creative, but some persons develop it, and some do not. Note that the foregoing perspectives reflect a shift of focus from what is created by those who are gifted to a potential for creativity which all humans have. My response to the foregoing shift in the view of what is essential to creativity is as follows: While I believe that all humans have a potential for creativity, I hold that any view or explanation of creativity has to take due account of genius, and also of brilliance, to a lesser degree, and that the rarity of these levels of creativity suggests that there is a difference in the potential for creativity.

In order to accommodate the view that each person has a potential for creativity, and the view that genius, and even brilliance, are rare gifts, I suggest that we consider a spectrum of creative ability. Given this view, there is a potential or capacity for creativity, with which, we assume humans are born. However, the creative ability of persons ranges from imaginative to inventive, and from inventive to ingenious. Within the ingenious range, we judge some individuals to be brilliant, and in rare cases, we judge some individuals to be geniuses. In both cases, we base our judgments on their creations. Also, although the criteria for the judgment is similar for brilliant and genius, the expected degree of originality, value, and effect is not as high for a person we take to be brilliant as it is for a person considered to be a genius. Finally, the creative intellect of the genius is such that she or he is able to produce that which is radically new or different, and that which has far-reaching effects and/or value.

Generally speaking, the greater the degree of genius, the greater the gulf of understanding between that person and the masses is likely to be. This gulf accounts for the fact that many geniuses are not recognized or appreciated in their own time. William Blake is an excellent example of such a genius, and there are many others, from the arts, sciences, humanities, etc.[4] Sadly, there are no doubt, some geniuses whose work has been lost, and also some whose work has not, as yet, been recognized.

Since all humans have a potential to create, but very few are gifted with genius, the degree of ability to create, as the degree of ability to reason, seems to be determined by one's potential. However, as with the ability to reason, because humans have a much greater capacity for creativity than they use, there can be high levels of creativity reached by those who are not gifted with brilliance or genius.

Given the foregoing view that creativity is an ability which ranges in degree from a simple potential to the expression of genius, let me offer a definition of "creativity" which is broad enough to accommodate this range. The definition of "creativity" which I propose is: (1) the ability to visualize or foresee and generate ideas, and the expressions or creations thereof, which are original. "Original," in this context, ranges from imaginative to inventive, and from inventive to ingenious; and (2) is of effect and/or value.

Having set forth a definition and description of creativity, let me, at least, mention the fact that research as to the cause or causes of creativity is ongoing. Also, we are only beginning to understand the complex workings of the human mind, let alone the most advanced forms of human thought. So, although there are current scientific studies, and a number of speculative explanations as to the nature and causes of creativity, we are far from understanding what causes it.[5]

It does seem clear that creativity needs to be encouraged and taught in schools. Such is the case not only because society needs to have creative minds, if it is to flourish, but individuals need to develop and express their creativity in order to lead meaningful, satisfying lives. To explore the problems of teaching creativity would take me afield of my objectives. Therefore, suffice it to say that hiring creative thinkers as teachers of creativity, and adopting methods of teaching which promote creativity are essential, if educators are concerned to help students develop their creative abilities. Also, students need to be taught to distinguish merely eccentric or erratic expressions from creative expressions which are, almost always, in response to, or the outgrowth of, an understanding of a particular subject matter.

Focusing again on the nature of creativity, let me reiterate that: 1. creativity can be defined as the ability to visualize or foresee and generate ideas, and the expressions or creations thereof, which are original, i.e., imaginative, inventive, or ingenious; and 2. of effect and/or value. Given my account of creativity, the potential for creativity is inherent in all humans, but that potential differs, so that one's developed creative ability can fall in a range from simple expressions of imagination to ingenious expressions which have a profound effect upon mankind.

Given the foregoing definition and account of creativity, let me turn now to the role of intuition, i.e., creative insight, in creativity.

The Role of Creative Insight in Creativity

Recall that in Chapter II, creative insight was described as an insight into either:

(1) a chain of links or transitions which may lead to the solution of some problem, or an explanation of the links; or
(2) a series of events which can lead to an eventuality.

With regard to mathematics even at an advanced level, creativity, in the form of discovery as well as problem solving, seems to involve the first form of creative insight, listed above.[6] However, most acts or expressions of creativity seems to involve the second form of creative insight, listed above, namely, an insight into a series of events which may lead to some eventuality. Also, as I stated, in Chapter II, the series of events may lead to a scientific discovery, a possible scientific explanation, an invention, a musical composition, or an artistic creation, etc.

Let us focus now on the role of creative insight in the creative process. To that end, I want to consider certain descriptions of the creative process put forth by two eminent scholars writing on the subject.

Two world renowned scholars, one a mathematician and one a scientist and philosopher wrote about the use of intuition in creativity. The great mathematician, Jules Henri Poincaré (1854–1912)[7] used the terms "illumination" and "intuition" to refer to what I have identified as creative insight.[8] Michael Polanyi (1891–1976), the well-known scientist and philosopher,[9] made clear that his notion of intuition could be likened to Poincaré's notion of illumination.[10]

Poincaré focused more on the function and/or use of illumination or intuition in mathematical discovery than on the nature of intuition itself, although he did consider it. Polanyi, on the other hand, focused both on the nature of intuition and its use and/or function in mathematical and scientific discovery and problem solving. As we shall see, neither scholar made the distinction which I have between the intuitive process, in general, involving a particular focus of concern, and the creative insight which is the culmination of that process. However, their descriptions of how intuition functions in mathematics and science support my account.

Jules Henri Poincaré

Let us first consider what Poincaré said about intuition, and then see how he described its use in mathematics. Poincaré, as I stated earlier, sometimes referred to intuition as illumination. He also referred to it as a feeling, and an inspiration.[11] Again, Poincaré focused on the use or function of intuition in mathematical creativity. Mathematical creativity, for Poincaré, seems clearly to have been the ability to choose those mathematical combinations which lead one to the discovery of mathematical law.[12] This choosing was, for Poincaré, an invention. Furthermore, this ability to invent, which is made possible by intuition, is not possessed by everyone. Regarding this subject Poincaré said:

> "We know that this feeling, this intuition of mathematical order, that makes us divine hidden harmonies and relations cannot be possessed by everyone. Some will not have this delicate feeling so difficult to define, or a strength of memory and attention beyond the ordinary, and then they will be absolutely incapable of understanding mathematics. Such are the majority.

Others will have this feeling only in a slight degree, but they will be gifted with an uncommon memory and a great power of attention. They will learn by heart the details one after another; they can understand mathematics and sometimes make applications, but they cannot create. Others, finally, will possess in a less or greater degree the special intuition referred to, and then not only can they understand mathematics even if their memory is nothing extraordinary, but they become creators and try to invent with more or less success according as this intuition is more or less developed in them. In fact, what is mathematical creation? It does not consist in making new combinations with mathematical entities already known. Anyone could do that, but the combinations so made would be infinite in numbers and most of them absolutely without interest. To create consists precisely in not making useless combinations and in making those which are useful and which are only a small minority. Invention is discernment, choice."[13]

With regard to intuition, or invention, Poincaré distinguishes two sequential phases which take place in mathematical creativity. The first is what he describes as long unconscious work [on a problem], i.e., work which takes place prior to intuition; the second is a sudden illumination or intuition. The intuition is dependent upon the unconscious work. However, in Poincaré's description of this process, the unconscious work is, in turn, the result of conscious research, reasoning etc. Poincaré describes the process in the following passage:

"Most striking at first is this appearance of sudden illumination, a manifest sign of long, unconscious prior work. The role of this unconscious work in mathematical invention appears to me incontestable, and traces of it would be found in other cases where it is less evident. Often when one works at a hard question, nothing good is accomplished at first attack. Then one takes a rest, longer or shorter, and sits down anew to do the work. During the first half-hour, as before, nothing is found, and then all of a sudden the decisive idea presents itself to the mind. It might be said that the conscious work has been more fruitful because it has been interrupted and the rest has given back to the mind its force and freshness. But it is more probable that the rest has been filled out with unconscious work and that the result of this work has afterward revealed itself to the geometer just as in the cases I have cited, only the revelation, instead of coming during a walk or journey, has happened during a period of conscious work, but independently of this work which plays at most a role of excitant, as if it were the goad stimulating the results already reached during rest, but remaining unconscious, to assume the conscious form."[14]

In another passage of his writings about the unconscious work of the mind in the creative process, Poincaré says:

"There is another remark to be made about the conditions of this unconscious work; it is possible, and of a certainty it is only fruitful, if it is on the one hand preceded and the other hand followed by a period of conscious work. These sudden inspirations . . . never happen except after some days of voluntary effort which has appeared absolutely fruitless and whence nothing good seems to have come, where the way taken seems totally astray. These efforts then have not been as sterile as one thinks; they have set agoing the unconscious machine and without them it would not have moved and would have produced nothing."[15]

Focusing on Poincaré's two phases of creative intuition as it occurs in mathematical discovery, I offer the following explanation of these phases in the light of my account of the intuitive process which culminates in an act of insight. First,

I will consider what I think he would say, and then I will give my response.

I think that what Poincaré took to be the first phase of intuition, he would view as an intermediary step between what I have identified as the integral intuitive process and the creative insight itself. This is the case because obviously Poincaré viewed the unconscious work, which he sometimes called "the unconscious effort of imagination" as independent of any conscious reasoned activity. Yet, it would seem to me that some reason is involved in the very possible combinations of ideas, even though this process is attributed to imagination, and is unconscious. In fact, I would suggest that it is part of the relating of present impressions to related memories. Hence, I would include the unconscious effort of imagination with the integral process which culminates in an act of insight.

Michael Polanyi

Let us turn now to Michael Polanyi's thought on the creative process, and the influence of Poincaré's thought on Polanyi's account of that process. Before giving Polanyi's views regarding the creative process, I think it is important to note that Carl Rogers, the world renowned psychotherapist, said that Polanyi was considered by many to be the premier scientist-philosopher of the twentieth century.[16]

As I noted earlier in this chapter, Polanyi made clear that he was influenced by Poincaré's account of intuition. In fact, Polanyi accepted much of Poincaré's account of illumination, i.e., intuition[17] (Polanyi also used the expression "creative insight" in reference to intuition used in the creative process. However, as we shall see, his account of the process differs from mine, even though it supports my account). In speaking about the use of intuition in scientific inquiry, Polanyi said:

"Intuition as I understand it, ranges widely. It stands for integrative acts taking place at any stage of scientific inquiry, from start to finish. The scientist's intuitive powers consist first in the faculty for surmising with a fair degree of probability the presence of a hidden coherence in nature. It is this faculty that espies a problem, the pursuit of which the scientist may accept as his task. The inquiry goes ahead then, guided by a series of surmises, which also have a reasonable chance of being right. This discovery is reached or may be reached – which solves a problem."[18]

In his book, *Personal knowledge: Towards a Post-Critical Philosophy*, Polanyi wrote about the use of intuition in mathematical discoveries. Regarding the subject, he said:

"I have shown how all the proofs and theorems of mathematics have been originally discovered by relying on their intuitive anticipation; how the established results of such discoveries are properly taught, understood, remembered in the form of their intuitively grasped outline; how these results are effectively reapplied and developed further by pondering their intuitive content; and that they can therefore gain our legitimate assent only in terms of our intuitive approval."[19]

Polanyi, as Poincaré had done, gave an account of two phases of intuition which were sharply separated. The second phase, according to Polanyi, occurred several hours after the first had ceased. The first involved the sweep of the imagination by a faculty for surmising the probability of a hidden coherence in nature; the second was when a bright idea turned up.[20]

In general, Poincaré's account of illumination, and Polanyi's account of intuition, as it occurs in the intuitive process, and the insight leading to a discovery or the solution of a problem, is consistent with my account of the kind of intuition which I have identified as creative insight. However, what Poincaré took to be the unconscious effort of the imagination, and Polanyi described as a sweep of the imagination by a faculty for surmising the probability of a hidden coherence in nature which involves selecting one possibility over others,[21] I would liken to the last step of the integral intuitive process in which present impressions are brought together with related memories. I say this because it seems clear to me that reason is involved in what Polanyi describes as the selecting of one possibility over others. Again, I hold this to be the case even if the reasoning is on an unconscious level, as Poincaré suggests. Recall that given my account of intuition, reason is involved in the process itself, but not in the act of insight in which the process culminates.

In addition to what I have said above about Poincaré's and Polanyi's accounts of intuition, it is important to note that the time between what Poincaré referred to as "the first and second phases of intuition" varies. According to some accounts, the time is less than a few hours, but according to many accounts, the time can vary between hours, days, weeks, months, or even years.[22]

Before leaving the subject of Polanyi's view of what I take to be "creative insight," I think it is worthy of note that in an essay about Polanyi's philosophy, Edward Pols likened the creative vital feature of Polanyi's notion of intuition to Henri Bergson's vital force.[23] He said this because Polanyi sometimes described what he called "tacit knowing," i.e., the intuitive aspect of knowing, to a plunging force.[24] Polanyi distinguished this intuitive kind of knowing from critical reasoning. Recall that Bergson had also distinguished intuitive ways of knowing of life from what he called the "intellect."[25] As I have made clear throughout this book, I do not agree that intuition is a non-discursive form or independent way of gaining knowledge. In my judgment, intuition is only one means to knowledge.

In addition to Poincaré and Polanyi, there are a number of scholars who have described creativity in such a way that it supports my account of creative insight.[26] However, since none of these descriptions, which I have read, involve the kind of philosophical analysis which Poincaré or Polanyi offered, I shall not here consider them. Nonetheless, it is interesting in reading such accounts that some of the creative insights come completed, and some come in dream states, and some just seem to unfold.[27]

ENDNOTES

1. From about the eighteenth century, the term "genius" came to mean a person endowed with superior creative powers. *Genius: The History of an Idea*, ed. by Penelope Murray, Oxford, England, Basil Blackwell, Ltd., c. 1989, pp. 1–2, and 7; and *Creativity: Paradoxes and Reflections*, ed. by Harry A. Wilmer, preface by Linus Pauling, p. 8.

2. Essential to the conception of genius is that the creation be of lasting quality and value. *Genius: The History of an Idea*, p. 7.

3. *Ibid.*, pp. 2–7.

4. In the area of art, the gulf does not seem to be so great. I think it is amazing and wonderful that the genius of Paul Klee, the great modern artist and contemporary of Pablo Picasso, could be recognized in his own lifetime.

5. We also do not understand why a number of highly creative people seem to suffer from some form of mental disturbance (The level of that disturbance also varies considerably). At this point in time, all we can do is look to science, primarily biology and psychology, for future insight into this subject.

6. With regard to mathematics, I think that what one says about creative insight rests, in large measure, upon the metaphysical view which one holds regarding whether mathematical truths exist independently of being known, or whether they are simply part of a constructed system. For my part, I tend to hold a Platonic view that the truths do exist, hence they are discoverable, not invented. However, a theory of explanation can be invented or constructed (Perhaps this is what Jules Henri Poincaré meant when he spoke of the creative insight into the laws of mathematics as inventions). Ultimately, of course, the question as to the nature of creative insight in mathematics has to rest with the mathematicians.

7. *Encyclopedia of Philosophy*, Book 6, p. 360. Most text books do not mention the name "Jules."

8. Henri Poincaré, "Mathematical Creation," in *The Creative Process*, ed. by Brewster Ghisetin, pp. 35–38.

9. *Carl Rogers: Dialogues*, ed. by Howard Kirschenbaum and Valerie Land Henderson, p. 154.

10. Michael Polanyi, *Knowing and Being*, p 201.
11. *The Creative Process*, pp. 35–38.
12. Ibid., p. 35–42.
13. Ibid., p. 35.
14. Ibid., p. 38.
15. Ibid.
16. *Carl Rogers Dialogues*, p. 154.
17. Michael Polanyi, *Knowing and Being*, pp. 210-202, and 204.
18. Ibid., p. 201.
19. Michael Polanyi, *Personal Knowledge: Towards a Post-Critical Philosophy*, p. 188.
20. Michael Polanyi, *Knowing and Being*, p. 201.
21. Ibid.
22. Sometimes these insights seem more like openings, or what Heidegger refers to as openness. After several years of struggling with various notions of revelation (which I will discuss in chapter V), I had an insight into their relatedness. Again, I would describe this as a kind of openness, but in this case, it was not full openness. After reflection on the experience which seemed to come "out of the blue," I have come to think of revelation as the self revealing to itself: 1. what is presented or given in experience, in light of one's self-development; or 2. the state of one's own self-development.
23. Edward Pols, "Polanyi and the Problem of Metaphysical Knowledge," in *Intellect and Hope*, ed. by Thomas A. Langford and William H. Poteat, p. 66.
24. Ibid.
25. Henri Bergson, *The Creative Mind*, pp. 29-47, 78-82.
26. To name a few of these scholars: Linus Pauling, "A Scientist," in *Creativity: Paradoxes & Reflections*, p. 83; Rudyard Kipling, "Working Tools" in the *Creative Process*, ed. by Brewster Ghiselin, pp. 157-159; John Hyde Preston, "A Conversation with Gertrude Stein," in the *Creative Process*, pp. 159-160; Henry Miller, "Reflections on writing," in the *Creative Process*, p. 180; Friedrich Nietzsche, "Composition of *Thus Spoke Zarathustra*, in the *Creative Process*, pp. 201-203; Carl Gustav Jung, "Psychology and Literature," in the *Creative Process*, pp. 226-251; James Engell, "Investigators of Genius: Gerard (Alexander) and Duff (William), in *The Creative Imagination*, pp. 78-87; Vincent Tomes, "Creativity in Art," in *Creativity in the Arts*, ed. by Vincent Tomes, pp. 97-109; Herbert Spencer, "Conversation with George Eliot, in the *Creative Process*, pp. 224-225.

27. Apparently, for Wolfgang Amadeus Mozart, and the mathematician Jacques Hadamard, insight came completed (Please see "a Letter," by Mozart, in the *Creative Process*, pp. 44-45, and the Introduction to the *Creative Process*, by Brewster Ghiselin, p. 15.). For Morton Prince, a writer, they came in dreams (Please see "Subconscious Intelligence Underlying Dreams," by Morton Prince, in the *Creative Process*, pp. 204-208.

CHAPTER V

TRANSCENDENT SPACE: A REGION OF TRANSCENDENT AWARENESS

It is this last chapter which for so long presented a stumbling block to me. For what seemed an interminable amount of time, but was really only several years (off and on), I struggled with the subject matter of this chapter, which I then viewed as the use of intuition in the mystical or spiritual experience. The problem which I faced was that there were so many accounts of the mystical or spiritual experience, both Western and non-Western accounts, which, for the most part, were reflective of a particular religious belief system.[1] I did avoid the foregoing problem in an article published in a scholarly journal,[2] wherein I gave an explanation of the mystical experience apart from any particular religious context. I explained the mystical experience by an analogy to Heidegger's account of revealed Being. However, it was not until I was doing research for a paper on Transcendence, which I was invited to give,[3] that I had the insight that my notion of intuition, as penetrative insight, and Heidegger's notion of revealed Being, i.e., what is given in experience, together form what Heidegger might have called "transcendent space" or "a region of transcendent awareness."

I have long known that transcendent awareness is needed to substantiate any belief in an Ultimate or ultimate reality. Also, I have known that only intuition and/or revelation can account for any awareness of that which is transmundane.[4]

Given what I have said about transcendence and transcendent awareness, my objectives in writing this chapter are: (1) to present the view that revelation, as viewed by Martin Heidegger, and intuition, i.e., penetrative insight, as I have described it, together form the space of transcendence, or a region of transcendent awareness; and (2) to show how via transcendent awareness, it is possible to understand some aspects of transcendence, in general, and to gain some insight into ultimate reality.

Prior to explaining transcendent space or awareness, it will be necessary for me to briefly review my account of intuition, especially, penetrative insight, and to present Heidegger's notion of revelation. However, before presenting that notion, I will briefly consider several other views of the subject.

Intuition as Penetrative Insight

With regard to intuition, I have explained why intuition, as it is generally understood in Western philosophical circles, has fallen into a state of disrepute. Also, I have given another account of intuition, which legitimates its use in "the life of the mind."

Intuition, as I explained in Chapter II, is an integral process of the mind which culminates in an act of insight. The process is grounded in reason, as reason forms part of the memories relating to the understanding of any subject. However, the act of insight in which the process culminates does not involve reason.

I identified two types of intuition, one penetrative, and the other creative. It is penetrative insight with which I am concerned in this chapter. Recall that at a mundane level, penetrative insight is an insight into either the structure of some problem, or a situation or condition. In Heidegger's ontology, insight would be into the Being Revealed to Dasein, i.e., human beings who are capable of understanding what is revealed. Throughout the book, I have referred to the Being revealed as Revealed Being.

At a level beyond the mundane, penetrative insight is an insight into the threshold of Revealed Being. Actually, as we shall see when I discuss Heidegger's notions of revelation, this is a region at the shifting horizon of Dasein's limit of understanding, which nonetheless involves awareness of the shifting of Being from revelation to concealment. The level of penetrative insight involved in this awareness must be developed.

Regarding the aforementioned development, as I explained in Chapter I, it was the view of Patañjali, the author of the ancient *Yoga Sūtra*, that what he called "supra-normal insight," requires moral, physical, and spiritual disciplines which prepare one for yoga proper which is a discipline involving stilling of the fluctuations of the mind that arise because of contact with the physical or material world. What I did not mention in Chapter I, is that there are three stages of yoga proper, namely: (i) *dhāraṇā*, i.e., fixed attention; (ii) *dhyāna*, i.e., meditation, which is the state of focusing on the continuous flow of similar mental modifications in that place of fixed attention; and (iii) *samādhi*, i.e., concentration or trance, which is that state wherein only the object of meditation "shines forth" in the mind, as though devoid of the thought of even the self who is meditating.[5] Furthermore, when the three states of dhāraṇā, dhyāna, and samādhi are combined, one achieves a state of saṁyama, which means constraint of the fluctuations of the mind that presupposes a discernment thereof.[6]

What is important for our purposes is that according to the *Yoga Sūtra*, upon achieving the state of saṁyama, the powers of intuition arise.[7] This is intuition as a seeing into, i.e., Darśana, which is actually the pure light of the true self, i.e. pure consciousness, unobstructed by sensations and thoughts from the material world, shinning forth. According to Patañjali, it is via this shinning that one gains, by stages, knowledge of the transcendent, and supernatural powers. I will not consider the powers, as they are not germane to this study, and as far as knowledge is concerned, let it suffice to say that it includes seeing into, i.e., knowledge of: past, present, and future events, other minds, the subtle and concealed, rebirth, and ultimately, total knowledge of reality.[8]

Although most Hindu schools of philosophy accept a belief

in yoga practice, and the intuitive powers of those advanced yogins, it is doubtful that most modern humans who are not Hindus could accept the account of intuitive powers attributed to the yogins,[9] let alone the belief in self-realization involving rebirth. Nor would most non-Hindus subscribe to the rigorous disciplined life required of a yogin. Yet it seems to me that those of us seeking more insight into transcendence should take due account of about two thousand years given to the study and development of supra-normal intuition. However, as I have made clear, my view of penetrative insight does not rest on a belief in rebirth, nor a belief that insight is actually the true self revealing to its self different levels of reality. In my view, penetrative insight at a transcendent level is simply a more developed state of one kind of intuition having to do with the structures of reality or Being. However, I do agree with Patañjali that insight into the transcendent does require a disciplined life (moral, physical, and mental) and meditation.

Having discussed intuition, especially penetrative insight, let me turn now to a consideration of revelation.

Nature of Revelation

Turning to a consideration of various views of revelation, clearly, significant differences exist between monotheistic religious/ philosophical traditions and certain Hindu religious/ philosophical schools of thought. In particular, I want to note the differences between the Judeo/Christian view of revelation found in the Old Testament, and that of the Advaita Vedānta school of Hindu philosophy. In addition, I will explore Martin Heidegger's view of revelation, as it has opened a new way of thinking about the subject, albeit, rooted in the Judeo/ Christian tradition. Also, it is Martin Heidegger's view which has relevance to what I will say about transcendence.

Focusing first on the Judeo/Christian view of revelation, this view has profoundly influenced Western thought regarding the subject, even for those who can no longer accept any such notion.[10] Speaking in broad generalities, in the Judeo/

Christian view of revelation, it is God, the creator of the earth, and personal savior of human beings, who reveals Himself and His plans for humans, set forth in the covenant, to the prophets (literally those who speak for God). According to the covenant, God promises salvation and everlasting life, if one is judged worthy. This view involves a historical drama, hence, time is viewed as linear.

By contrast to the foregoing monotheistic view on revelation, the Advaita Vedānta view is that of Self-revelation or Self-realization,[11] which is necessary for the goal of *mokṣa*, i.e. release from rebirth. Because of the belief in rebirth, time is viewed as cyclical. Advaita Vedānta is a very influential school of Hindu philosophy which reflects a major stream of thought found in the sacred Hindu literature, namely, the *Vedas*. Advaita Vedānta is based on a unified ontology. In fact, one's true or real Self, i.e., Ātman, and the cosmic impersonal absolute reality, underlying the appearance of the physical world, i.e., Brahman, are taken to be identical.[12] The nature of Ātman and Brahman can never be captured because, as is the case with all ultimates, they transcend human categories of understanding. Hindus express this inability to understand when they say of the ultimate, *neti neti*, i.e., neither this nor that. However, one can experience the ultimate, and based on this experience, the ultimate is taken to be an impersonal absolute, the experience of which is described as *saccidānanda*. Unpacked, there are three key terms to consider: (1) *sat* - which is the stem of the term *satya*, i.e., truth (*sat* also conveys being or existence); (2) *cit* - which is the stem of the term *citta*, i.e., consciousness; and (3) *ānanda* - which means bliss. So, the Absolute is taken to be an all-pervasive state of consciousness and bliss which is both the nature of the true Self, Ātman, and the cosmic reality, Brahman, that underlies the appearance of the natural world.

In coming to realize Ātman, one also comes to realize Brahman, as they are the same. However, the realization of Ātman, i.e., Self-realization, is an experience which involves many lifetimes and great effort and discipline. The effort and

discipline are necessary in order to overcome the ego or
material self, which keeps one from Self-realization. The effort
includes: doing one's duty and living righteously, i.e., *dharma*;
following a yoga path or paths, which I mentioned in Chapter
I, (*bhakti yoga*, i.e., the path of devotion, *karma yoga*, i.e., the
path of good works, and *jñāna yoga*, i.e., a spiritual kind of
knowledge which presupposes both a high level of reasoning
power and moral development); and yoga proper which is
described in the section on intuition. Given the foregoing
sketch of Advaita Vedānta metaphysics, I think it is clear why
revelation is Self (the true Self)–revelation.

Having adumbrated revelation from the perspective of the
Advaita Vedānta school of thought, let us turn now to a
consideration of revelation within Heidegger's thought. What
revelation is and how it functions in Heidegger's philosophy
is more complex than in the other two views being considered. This is due, in part, to the nature of revelation, including the shifting horizons of Being Itself, which I shall explain,
and the shifting horizons of human understanding and/or
awareness of what is revealed.

As to the nature of revelation, in the works of Heidegger,
one can say that what is revealed is Being, i.e. Revealed Being,
(described in Chapter III)[13] which is what is presented or
given, *es gibt*, in experience to *Dasein*, i.e., human beings as
the place where Being is revealed. Hence, there is no Revealed
Being without Dasein. *Dasein* has as its essence, the capacity
or potentiality to understand what is given.[14] However, Dasein
can be aware of that which transcends understanding.

Focusing first on understanding, as I explained earlier in
Chapter III, for Heidegger, understanding involves a relation
between the Being which is given or revealed and Dasein as
the place where Being is given. However, one's level of
understanding is based primarily on her or his openness, i.e.,
receptivity, or the lack thereof, to the given. Also, the horizons
of one's understanding shift, due to such influences as mood,[15]
level of authenticity,[16] interest, and apparently even such
considerations as the state of one's health.

Making a transition from understanding to awareness, not only can Dasein become aware of the shifting horizons of her or his own understanding, but, as Heidegger suggested, one can become aware of the shift from the presencing to distancing of Being itself.[17] "Being itself" refers to what Heidegger called the "Being of Beings,"[18] which includes both the Being which is revealed, and that which is unrevealed. A number of scholars take the unrevealed to be the source of what is revealed,[19] or as what I described in my doctoral dissertation that by which all things emerge into presence and endure.[20]

Being Itself would also appear to be what Heidegger refers to as "That Which Regions."[21] According to Heidegger, a region is a focus of concern in which beings and things come to have meaning, and one's regions make up her or his world.[22] Hence, "That Which Regions" would seem to be the source of human regioning or Being itself. Be that as it may, part of the Being of Beings is revealed, and part is unrevealed. What humans can be aware of is the shifting horizons of what is revealed, i.e., *es gibt.* "Presencing and Distancing of Being" is an expression which describes the revelation and withdrawing of Being itself. Also, whereas variations in the presencing of Being can be noted in history, it is via awareness that we can say that this is an age in which there is a distancing of Being. Examples which Heidegger gave of when more of Being was revealed were at the time of the Greeks, the Jewish prophets, and Jesus.[23] By contrast, according to Heidegger, this is an age in which Being is withdrawing.[24]

The subject of the presencing and distancing of Being is a difficult part of Heidegger's ontology. However, I think that it holds the key to deeper insights into transcendence than some scholars writing on the subject have thought possible. Let us turn now to the subject of transcendence, i.e., transcendent space or awareness.

Transcendence

Before I give an account of transcendence, I want to state the parameters, as well as the guidelines for my view of the subject. First, I think that it is important to state what is an obvious, but often unstated truth regarding the subject of transcendence, namely, that the philosophical theories, having to do with transcendence, have, in general, reflected a particular philosopher's or theologian's fundamental metaphysical and/or epistemological beliefs as well as her/his values regarding transcendence. Furthermore, as is well-known, these beliefs and values are context dependent, i.e., they have to do with cultural, linguistic, and religious contexts. Such being the case, I think it is important for those of us seeking truth, in the Heideggerian sense of the unconcealedness of Being, to heed the spirit of what Thomas Huxley had to say about the guidelines for seeking truth or knowledge. Thomas Huxley, the contemporary of Darwin, and champion of his views, who was the grandfather of Sir Julian Huxley and Aldous Huxley, said:

> What I have to do is to induce my intense desire to take due account of the facts, not to force the facts into agreement with my wishes. . . . Accept a fact as a little child does. Be prepared to give up every preconceived idea . . . . Follow nature humbly wherever, into whatever abysses she may lead you, or you will learn nothing.[25]

Broadening Huxley's Weltenschauung, let us take "facts" to be phenomena, or what presents itself to us in our experience, and "nature" to be that area of awarenesss which encompasses, but transcends Heidegger's notion of understanding as a relation between what is presented or given in experience, *es gibt*, and humans as the place where the given is revealed, *Dasein*.[26]

If as suggested, instead of facts, we focus on phenomena, and hold that nature extends to the horizon of awareness, and we realize the traps that many philosophers have fallen into because of preconceived ideas and accepted belief systems, then I think that we have an idea of the "tight rope" which must be "walked," if one is not, on the one-hand to claim too much regarding transcendence, or, on the other-hand to disregard or reject any meaningful consideration of the subject.

How Insight and Revelation Lead to Transcendence

At the outset of this chapter, I stated that I took transcendence to be the space where revelation and intuition come together. Later, I said that revelation and intuition form the space of transcendence. To be more specific, I think that intuition as it penetrates what is revealed, forms the space of transcendence. By intuition, I mean that penetrative insight into Being at the threshold of revelation which I described in the section on intuition. Also, I presuppose, as do the Hindu philosophers, that this kind of insight is the result of the development of moral character, a physically and mentally disciplined life, and meditation. By revelation, I mean Heidegger's sense of the given, i.e., *es gibt*, as described in the section on revelation. However, we need to keep in mind both the shifting horizons of one's understanding which at the horizon or limit still allows awareness, and what Heidegger takes to be a shift of Being itself in its presencing and distancing, and hence, revelation and concealment by withdrawal.

Given what I have said as to the nature of intuition and revelation, when and where intuition penetrates what is revealed forms the space of transcendence. If one views penetrative insight as covering a range from the mundane to the trans-mundane, then trans-mundane or transcendent awareness could include areas of finite existence, such as Karl Jaspers, a philosopher and contemporary of Martin Heidegger, described, i.e., rising to states beyond the things in the world and the public perspective,[27] and the state of one's true being which is glimpsed from a frontier or horizon.[28] However, as I believe I have made clear, it is penetrative insight into Being at the threshold of revelation with which I am concerned here. Hence, the transcendence of which I speak would be at the shifting edge of the horizon of understanding, where there still can be an awareness of the shifting threshold of the revelation of Being Itself. As I have explained what is revealed at a given time is due to the presencing or distancing of Being Itself.

Whereas Karl Jasper sometimes spoke as if we conjure up or construct the transcendental realm,[29] it is not a construction in Heidegger's thought. Rather, it is a possibility, and even an expectation that at some future time, as has occurred in the past, Being will reveal more of itself.[30] Thus, we have Heidegger, in *Gelassenheit* (*Discourse on Thinking*), describing an active waiting for unrevealed Being,[31] with a sense of thankfulness or appreciation, i.e., *dankbar*,[32] an openness, and a letting-be or releasement, i.e., *gelassenheit*,[33] which means that we do not try to force categories of understanding (form concepts or reason about) on that which cannot be understood – at least until it reveals more of itself.

According to Heidegger's belief in the presencing and distancing of Being itself, and his account of waiting for Being to reveal itself, there is, on the one hand, the inability to understand what is not revealed, but also, on the other hand, some awareness of, hope for, and even expectation of, more revelation of Being. Of course, if there is more revelation, and one is receptive to that revelation, more awareness, and perhaps even some understanding of it is possible.

Given my account of penetrative insight, it is possible to penetrate those transcendent levels of awareness of Being. Thus, given penetrative insight, and more of a presencing of Being, the possibility of greater awareness, and perhaps even some understanding, of that Being is possible.

Should one be dissatisfied with what can be learned about Being, i.e., reality, via the active waiting which Heidegger describes, recall that he believed that more of Being was revealed in the past, i.e., at the times of the Greeks, the Jewish prophets, and Jesus. Obviously, Heidegger's world view was Western. Focusing simply on the axis age, had he considered non-Western as well as Western traditions, he would have included not only the Jewish prophets, but Confucius, Lao Tzu, and Buddha.

It seems to me that were humans to study all of the accounts of the Ultimate from around the world, based on accounts of intuition and/or revelation, we might indeed have some better understanding of Being or the Ultimate. Of course, the ancient Jain adage – of several blind-folded persons describing an elephant from different vantage points – might apply. Nevertheless, focusing on the means to knowledge, instead of an analysis of the differences in metaphysics, it seems to be the time to compare the insights of seers and revelations of the prophets or self-realized individuals, from all traditions, to see what we can learn about the views of the Ultimate. Also, given Heidegger's account of understanding which is not mind-dependent, we have an epistemological basis for what the Hindus call *Darśana*, i.e, "seeing into" transcendence.

SUMMARY

In this final chapter of the book, I have suggested that transcendence can be viewed as the space formed when intuition penetrates what is revealed. Also, although I considered other views regarding revelation, it is the Heideggerian view which I consider relevant to this view of transcendence. Intuition, as I described it, is an integral process of the mind which culminates in an act of insight. While the process is grounded in reason, the insight does not involve reason. I distinguished two kinds of insight, namely, penetrative and creative. On a mundane level, penetrative insight can be described as insight into the structure of a problem or a situation or condition, but, also, on a higher level, there is what I have described as penetrative insight into the threshold of Revealed Being. This is the kind of insight with which the ancient Hindu Yoga School of Philosophy was concerned. According to the Yoga School, what they called "supranormal insight" requires moral, physical, and spiritual discipline which prepares one for the discipline of Yoga proper, i.e., the stages of fixed attention, meditation, and trance or concentration, which when combined bring forth saṁyama, i.e., constraint of the fluctuations of the mind. When saṁyama is achieved, the intuitive powers having to do with the transcendent arise.

Although the goal of the Yoga discipline is Self-realization, and according to Hindu beliefs, this realization takes many lifetimes, one does not have to accept this metaphysics in order to appreciate the belief that at a very advanced stage of what we call "meditation," intuitive powers into the transcendent arise, and that this advanced stage requires a disciplined life (morally, physically, and mentally) involving meditation.

Again, given the foregoing meanings of "intuition" and "revelation" (in the Heideggerian sense), I have suggested that transcendence is that space formed by intuition, i.e., penetrative insight, into the threshold of Being Itself which is at the shifting edge of awareness.

Finally, I have argued that given Heidegger's belief in the presencing and distancing of Being itself, and my account of penetrative insight, it is indeed possible to gain a deeper awareness, and possibly some understanding of Being itself. Of course this awareness is dependent upon both the development of intuitive powers and the presencing of Being.

ENDNOTES

1. Even those accounts which try to explain the experience itself, as one of communion or unity, seem to leave us on the horns of a dilemma based on either a monotheistic view of reality wherein God is the ultimate other, or monistic views of reality, such as Advaita Vedānta, wherein it makes sense to claim Tat-tvam-asi (that thou art). Also, it does not help that some mystics such as Meister Eckhart, who was steeped in the monotheistic view of the Roman Catholic Church, spoke of the ultimate in terms of unity. Also, as I indicated in the Introduction to the book, intuition, or the results thereof, cannot be based on a particular religious or metaphysical view. On the contrary, as I argue in this chapter, it is intuition and revelation which make possible awareness and perhaps some understanding of reality.

2. Hope Fitz, "The Mystical Experience from a Heideggerian Perspec-

tive," in *The Journal of Religious Studies*, Vol. XVII, Spring 1990, No. 1, pp. 51–59.

3. I was invited to speak by the Program Chairperson, Professor Stephen Erickson, of the Karl Jasper's Society of North America at the Eastern Division Meetings of the American Philosophical Association, the Marriott Hotel, New York, December 27–30, 1995.

4. Obviously, an appeal to sense experience, plus reason, in the limited sense of structuring what is given in sense experience, and deriving conclusions from premises, etc. cannot account for an awareness of that which is trans-mundane or transcendent.

5. *The Yoga System of Patañjali*, tr. from Sanskrit by James Haughton Woods, Book III, Supernormal Powers, Verse 1, pp. 204–205.

6. *Ibid.*, Verse 4, p. 205; and *Yoga Philosophy of Patañjali*, Book III, Verse 4, p. 253.

7. *The Yoga System of Patañjali*, Book III, Verse 5, p. 206 and Verse 17, p. 233.

8. *Ibid.*, Verses 16, 18, 19, 25, 35, and 54.

9. *Ibid.*

10. Of course, this is because the Judeo/Christian world view, including values as well as beliefs, has influenced social and legal systems, as well as language, i.e., symbols and signs, literature, and philosophical systems or movements, etc.

11. In addition to the *Vedānta Sūtras*, with commentary by Śaṅkara (One translation by George Thibaut is contained in the *Sacred Books of the East*, ed. by Max Muller, Volumes 34 and 38), there are also two good Western books on Advaita Vedānta, namely a *Source Book of Advaita Vedānta* by Eliot Deutsch and J. A. B. van Buitenen, Honolulu, The University Press of Hawaii, 1971, and *Advaita Vedānta*, by Eliot Deutsch, Honolulu, East-West Center Press, c. 1968.

12. This Advaitin view is based on the *Vedic* literature, such as: Chāndogya Upaniṣad, tr. by Swami Swahananda, in the Upaniṣad Series, Madras, Sri Ramakrishnan, third impression, 1975, 3.11.4, 3.14.1, 5.11.1, and the beautiful passages in Chapter VI, in which Śvetaketu is told repeatedly by his father that he is Ātman (tat tvam asi). If he is Ātman, then he is Brahman, 5.11.1.

13. Martin Heidegger, *Being and Time*, pp. 215 and 307; Martin Heidegger, *On Time and Being*, pp. 2–24; Martin Heidegger, *An Introduction to Metaphysics*, pp. 85–88.

14. Heidegger, *Being and Time*, pp. 34–35, and 182–193; Heidegger.

15.   Heidegger, *Being and Time*, p. 173, 179 and 228–235. Heidegger uses the term *angst*, which usually is translated as anxiety, in the sense of the basic mood, or root of moods. This is a complex notion, but basically, it is a feeling of being lifted from one's circumstances which brings about a change in one's perspective (point of view or attitude).

16.   *Ibid.*, pp. 228–229, 232, 234–235.

17.   Heidegger, *Discourse on Thinking*, pp. 66–67; Heidegger, "What are Poets For? in *Poetry, Language, and Thought*, pp. 91–97, and 117.

18.   Heidegger, "What are Poets For?" in *Poetry, Language and Thought*, pp. 100–102, 11 and 123; Heidegger, *What is Called Thinking*, pp. 235–238, and 244; Heidegger, in *The Question of Being*, p. 95; and Heidegger as quoted in *Through Phenomenology to Thought*, by William Richardson, S. J., p. 12.

19.   Scholars such a Professor Hubert Dreyfus, at Berkeley, focus on Being-in-the- world, hence his book by that title. However, in the famous book *Heidegger: Through Phenomenology to Thought*, by William J. Richardson, S. J., with a preface by Martin Heidegger, Richardson makes clear that he thinks Heidegger believes in a source, pp. 257, 446–447, and 459. Furthermore, as one moves to Heidegger's later writings, such as "Conversation on a Country Path," in *Discourse on Thinking*, pp. 65–81, it is clear to me that what Heidegger calls "that-which-regions" is a source.

20.   I based this description on the following: Lectures by Stephen A. Erickson, Professor of Philosophy, at Claremont Graduate School, 1977; and what is cited in endnote 18, above, plus, Martin Heidegger, *An Introduction to Metaphysics*, pp. 11–14; William J. Richardson, S. J., *Heidegger: Through Phenomenology to Thought*, p. 5. In the last two works cited, what is discussed is the early Greek meaning of the word *physis*. According to Heidegger, *physis*, which is usually translated as natural or physical, meant Being to the early Greeks. However, what the early Greeks meant by "Being" is what Heidegger called "Being of beings," and what I sometimes refer to as "Being-ness of beings."

21.   Heidegger, "Conversation on a Country Path," in *Discourse on Thinking*, pp. 70–88.

22.   Heidegger, *Being and Time*, pp. 136–148.

23.   Heidegger, *Poetry, Language, Thought*, p. 184.

24.   *Ibid.*

25.   Herbert Wendt, *In Search of Adam*, p. 263.

26. Stephen A. Erickson, *Language and Being: An Analytic Phenomenology*, p. 146.

27. Karl Jaspers, *Man in the Modern Age*, pp. 175, 178, and 181.

28. *Ibid.*, p. 195.

29. *Ibid.*, p. 175.

30. Heidegger, *Discourse on Thinking*, pp. 54–90; Hope Fitz, *Intuition as an Integral Process of the Mind*, Chapter III, pp. 80–87.

31. Heidegger, *Discourse on Thinking*, pp. 46–47, 53.

32. *Ibid.*, p. 85.

33. *Ibid.*, pp. 54–55, 66–70, 72–76, and 81–83.

A SUMMARY OF THE MAJOR IDEAS OF THE BOOK AND A POSTSCRIPT

In this book, I have had several major objectives:

1. to present the view that intuition is a natural and necessary part of the "mind's life" which needs to be developed.

2. to make clear that without an appeal to intuition, much of human experience is inadequately described or explained, and some is inexplicable, e.g., a justified belief in an ultimate reality.

3. to explain that traditional views of intuition, Western and Hindu, are not acceptable to rigorous thinkers, because intuition is taken to be a non-discursive form or independent way of gaining knowledge.

.. to present an account of the nature and uses of intuition which can be accepted by any rigorous thinker because it is not at odds with what knowledge is generally taken to be, namely, a discursive process of thought or the results thereof.

   (a) to argue that intuition is not a non-discursive form or independent way of gaining knowledge, but simply one means to knowledge, which is complementary to reason, and can be checked by reason.

   (b) to show that via the two kinds of intuition which I have identified, namely, penetrative insight, and creative insight, humans can account for a great deal of their experience which otherwise is either inadequately explained or inexplicable.

I believe and hope that I have accomplished my objectives. In addition, I believe that I have shown that intuition, as a

means to knowledge, can be accepted as evidence for justification of certain beliefs, thereby, expanding the criteria for
claims to knowledge.

Also, I have offered an account of creativity, which embraces aspects of both the old view according to which creativity was a gift of genius, and the more contemporary view
that all persons have a potential for creativity, but some
develop it and some don't. Given my view, all persons have
a potential for creativity, but the potential differs as to how
creative one can become. Based on the foregoing view, I
define creativity as: an ability to visualize or foresee and
generate the ideas and/or creations thereof which are original. Original ranges from imaginative to inventive, and from
inventive to ingenious, and is of effect and/or value.

Finally, I think that I have offered a novel view of transcendence, which is formed by intuition, i.e., penetrative
insight and the threshold of what Heidegger describes as the
shifting horizons of Revealed Being. I believe that this account
is important, because it makes possible a justification of beliefs
about the awareness and some understanding of an Ultimate
or ultimate reality.

Although, my account will not satisfy those who already
have very definite ideas about the nature of the Ultimate, or
those that seek them, I believe it to be truer to the situation
in which humans find themselves. I refer to that state of not
knowing the nature of the Ultimate, but having some insight
into and experiences of it, and even some understanding of
it. The understanding can come partly from one's own insight
and experience. However, I think that a great deal of understanding could be gained from the intercommunication
of so called "mystics," or highly intuitive people, from various
traditions around the world. Also, as I suggested earlier, given
Heidegger's epistemology, it would behoove scholars to
undertake a careful comparison of what the seers and/or
prophets, who wrote the sacred books, had to say about their
insights into the Ultimate.

BIBLIOGRAPHY

Dictionaries

A Concise Dictionary of Indian Philosophy (Sanskrit/English), by John Grimes, Madras, India, Radhakrishnan Institute for Advanced Study in Philosophy, First Published 1988.

The New Cassell's Dictionary of the German Language, New York, Funk and Wagnall, 1958.

The American Heritage Dictionary of the English Language, ed. William Morris, Boston, American Heritage Publishing Co., Inc., and Houghton Mifflin Company, 1969.

A Dictionary of Philosophy and Religion: Eastern and Western Thought, by William L. Reese, New Jersey, Humanities Press, c. 1980.

The Oxford Universal Dictionary on Historical Principles, Third Edition, prepared by William Little, H. W. Fowler, and J. Coulson; ed. C. T. Onions, Oxford, Clarendon Press, 1955.

Works By and About Scholars or Schools of Philosophy Dealing With Intuition

Advaita Vedānta

Vedānta Sūtras, with the commentary by Śaṅkarācārya, tr. by George Thibaut, in *Sacred Books of The East*, Part I in Vol. 34, ISBN 81-208-0135-0, Part II in Vol. 38, ISBN 81-208-0139-3, Delhi, Patna, Bangalore, Madras, Motilal Banarsidass, last printing 1988.

Deutsch, Eliot, *Advaita Vedānta: A Philosophical Reconstruction*, Honolulu, East-West Center Press, c. 1969.

Deutsch, Eliot, and van Buitenen, J. A. B., *A Source Book of Advaita Vedānta*, Honolulu, The University Press of Hawaii, c. 1971, ISBN 0-87022-189-2.

Bergson, Henri

Bergson, Henri, the essay "An Introduction to Metaphysics," in a booklet, tr. by T. E. Hulme, and Introduction by Thomas A. Goudge, New York, Macmillan Publishing Company, c. 1955, ISBN 0-02-358470-X.

Bergson, Henri, *Creative Evolution*, tr. Arthur Mitchell, Ph.D., New York, Henry Holt and Company, 1911.

Bergson, Henri, *The Creative Mind: An Introduction to Metaphysics*, tr. by Mabelle L Andison, New York, The Wisdom Library, A Division of Philosophical Library, c. 1946, ISBN 0-8065-0421-8.

Bergson, Henri, *The Two Sources of Morality and Religion*, tr. by R. Ashley Audra and Cloudesley Brereton, with the assistance of W. Horsfall Carter, Notre Dame, Indiana, University of Notre Dame Press, Third Printing 1986, ISBN 0-268-01835-9.

Lacey, A. R., *Bergson*, London and New York, Routledge, c. 1989, ISBN 0-415-08763-5.

Lovejoy, Arthur, O., *The Reason, The Understanding, and Time*, pp. 68-71, Baltimore, The Johns Hopkins Press, c. 1961.

Heidegger, Martin

Heidegger, Martin, *Poetry, Language, Thought*, tr. and Introduction by Albert Hofstadter, New York, Harper Colophon Books, Harper & Row Publishers, c. 1971.

Heidegger, Martin, *Existence and Being*, with an introduction and analysis by Werner Brock, South Bend, Indiana, Gateway Editions, Ltd., first American edition published 1949.

Patañjali and The Yoga School

Patañjali

Yoga Philosophy of Patañjali (the *Yoga Sūtra,* i.e., Patañjali's aphorisms in Sanskrit, with commentary by Vyāsa), tr., commentary, and annotations by Swami Hariharānanda Āranya, rendered in English by P. N. Mukerji, Albany, New York, State University of New York Press, 1981.

The Yoga-System of Patañjali (embracing the *Yoga Sūtras* of Patañjali, the comment by Vyāsa, and the explanation by Vācaspati-Misra,) tr. from the original Sanskrit by James Haughton Woods, Delhi, Varanasi, Patna, Motilal Banarsidass, 1983.

Puligandla, R, *Fundamentals of Indian Philosophy,* New Delhi, India, D. K. Print World Ltd. India edition, 1997.

Tigunait, Rajmani, Pandit, Ph.D., *Seven Systems of Indian Philosophy,* Homesdale, Pennsylvania, The Himalayan International Institute of Yoga Science and Philosophy, c. 1983.

Poincaré

Jules Henri Poincaré, "Mathematical Creation," in *The Creative Process,* ed. by Brewster Ghiselin, California, A Mentor Book, New American Library, c. 1952, by the Regents of the University of California, c. 1952.

Jules Henri Poincaré, *Science and Hypothesis,* with a preface by J. Larmor, New York, Doveer, Publications, Inc. c. 1952.

Polanyi

Intellect and Hope: Essays in the Thought of Michael Polanyi, ed. by Thomas Langford and William H. Poteat, Durham, North Carolina, Duke University Press, c. 1968.

Polanyi, Michael, *Knowing and Being,* essays by Michael Polanyi, ed. by Marjorie Grene, Chicago. The University of Chicago Press, c. 1969.

Polany, Michael, *Personal Knowledge: Towards a Post-Critical Philosophy,* one edition: Chicago, The University of Chicago Press, c. 1958; another edition: New York, Harper Torchbooks, The Academy Library, Harper & Row Publishers, c. 1964.

Rogers, Carl, "Dialogue With Michael Polanyi," in *Carl Rogers Dialogues,* Boston, Houghton Mifflin company, c 1989.

Radhakrishnan

The Philosophy of Sarvepalli Radhakrishnan, ed. by Paul Arthur Schilpp, New York, Tudor Publishing Company, c. 1952 by The Library of Living Philosophers, Inc.

Radhakrishnan, Sarvepalli, *An Idealist View of Life,* The Hibbert Lectures for 1929, London, George Allen & Unwin Ltd., Fifth Impression, (second edition), 1957.

Radhakrishnan, Sarvepalli, *Eastern Religions and Western Thought,* Delhi, London, New York, Oxford University Press, Fifth impression (paperback) 1993.

Radhakrishnan, Sarvepalli, *Radhakrishnan: Selected Writings on Philosophy, Religion and Culture,* ed., and with an Introduction by Robert A. McDermott, New York, E. P. Dutton and Company, Inc., c. 1970, ISBN 0-525-47268-1.

Radhakrishnan, Sarvepalli, *Religion and Culture,* Delhi, Published by Hind Pocket Books, c. 1968.

Works on Intuition Consulted But Not Used

Kitaro, Nishida, *Intuition and Reflection in Self-Consciousness,* tr. by Valdo H. Viglielmo, with Takeuchi Toshinori and Joseph S. O'Leary, New York, State University of New York Press, c. 1987, ISBN 0-88706-370-5.

Mehta, Rohit, *The Intuitive Philosophy: Krishnamurti's Approach to Life,* Bombay, Chetana, c. 1950.

Gardiner, Patrick, *Schopenhauer,* Baltimore, Md., Penguin Books, c. 1963.

Schopenhauer, Arthur, *The World as Will and Representation,* Vol. I and Vol. II, trl from the German by E. F. J. Payne, New York, Dover Publications, Inc., Vol. I, c. 1969, Vol II, first published 1966.

Vaughan, Frances E., *Awakening Intuition,* New York, Anchor Books Anchor Press/Doubleday, 1979, ISBN 0-385-13371-5.

Weissman, David, *Intuition and Ideality,* New York, State University of New York Press, c. 1987, ISBN 0-88706-428-0.

Dissertation on Intuition

Fitz, Hope K., *Intuition as an Integral Process of the Mind,* A Dissertation submitted to the Faculty of Claremont Graduate School in partial fulfillment of the requirements for the degree of Doctor of Philosophy in the Graduate Faculty of Individual Degrees (sub-field – East-West Comparative Philosophy), Claremont, 1981.

Works on Subjects Related to Intuition

Creativity

The Creative Process, ed. by Brewster Ghiselin, California, A Mentor Book, New American Library, c. 1952, by the Regents of the University of California.

Creativity in the Arts, ed. by Vincent Tomas, New Jersey, Prentice-Hall, Inc.c. 1964.

Creativity: Paradoxes & Reflections, ed. by Harry A. Wilmer, Preface by Linus Pauling, Wilmette, Illinois, Chiron Publications, c. 1991.

Engell, James *The Creative Imagination: Enlightenment to Romanticism,* Cambridge, Massachusetts, c. 1981, ISBN 0-674-17572-7.

Yukawa, Hideki, *Creativity and Intuition: A Physicist Looks at East and West,* tr. by John Bester, Tokyo, Kodansha International Ltd., 1973, ISBN 0-87011-177-9.

Genius

Genius, *The History of an Idea,* ed. by Penelope Murray, Oxford, England, Basil Blackwell Ltd., c. 1989, ISBN 0-631-15785-9.

The Creative Process, (see Creativity).

Revelation

Erickson, Stephen A., *Language and Being: An Analytic Phenomenology,* New Haven Connecticut, Yale University Press, c. 1970.

Heidegger, Martin

Heidegger, Martin, *An Introduction to Metaphysics,* tr. by Ralph Manheim, New York, Anchor Books, Doubleday & Company, Inc., 1961.

Heidegger, Martin, *Being and Time,* tr. by John Macquarrie & Edward Robinson, New York, Harper & Row Publishers, c. 1962.

Heidegger, Martin, *Discourse on Thinking,* a translation of *Gelassenheit,* by John M. Anderson and E. Hans Freund, with an Introduction by John M. Anderson, New York, Harper Torchbooks, Harper & Row Publishers, c. 1959.

Heidegger, Martin, *Existence and Being,* with an introduction and analysis by Werner Brock, South Bend, Indiana, Gateway Editions, Ltd., first American edition published 1949.

Heidegger, Martin, *On Time and Being,* tr. by Joan Stambaugh, New York, Harper Colophon Books, Harper & Row Publishers, c. 1972, ISBN: 0-6-090543-3.

Heidegger, Martin, *Poetry, Language, Thought,* tr. and Introduction by Albert Hofstadter, New York, Harper Colophon Books, Harper & Row Publishers, c. 1971.

Heidegger, Martin, *The Question of Being,* tr. and Introduction by Jean T. Wilde and William Kluback, New Haven, Connecticut, College & University Press, c. 1958.

Heidegger, Martin, *What is a Thing*, tr. by W. B. Barton, Jr., and Vera Deutsch, with an analysis by Eugene T. Gendlin, South Bend, Indiana, Gateway Editions, Ltd., c. 1967.

Heidegger, Martin, *What is Called Thinking*, tr. of *Was Heisst Denken?* by J. Glenn Gray, and with an Introduction by J. Glenn Gray, New York, Harper Colophon Books, Harper & Row Publishers, c. 1968.

Richardson, William J. Richardson, S.J., *Heidegger: Through Phenomenology to Thought*, Preface by Martin Heidegger, The Hague, Martinus Nijhoff, c. 1963.

Transcendence

Jaspers, Karl, *Man in the Modern Age*, tr. by Eden and Cedar Paul, New York, Doubleday & Co. Inc., c. 1957.

Right Brain/Left Brain Thinking

Wonder, Jacquelyn Wonder, and Donovan, Priscilla, *Whole-Brain Thinking*, New York, William Morrow and Company, Inc., c.1984, ISBN 0-688-02665-6.

Articles by Author Having to do With Intuition

Fitz, Hope K., "The Nature and Significance of Intuition in Patanjali's *Yoga Sūtra*, and in the Philosophical Writings of Radhakrishnan," published in *The Journal of Religious Studies*, Vol. xxvi, Spring-Autumn 1995, Punjabi University, Patiala [Punjab], India.

Fitz, Hope K., "The Role of Self-Discipline in the Process of Self-Realization," an article written with Dr. Bala Sunder Rai Bhalla, Reader at Punjabi University, India, published in *The Journal of Religious Studies*, Vol. XIX, Spring 1991, No. 1, Punjabi University, Patiala, [Punjab], India.

Fitz, Hope K., "The Mystical Experience From a Heideggerian Perspective," an article published in *The Journal of Religious Studies*, Vol. xviii, No. 1, Spring 1990, Punjabi University, Patiala [Punjab], India.

Fitz, Hope K., "The Nature and Significance of Intuition" (A View Based on a Core Idea Held by Radhakrishnan), an article published in *The Journal of Indian Council of Philosophical Research,* Vol. vi, Number 3, May – August, New Delhi, India. (This article was published in a book, *New Essays in the Philosophy of Sarvepalli Radhakrishnan,* ed. by S.S. Rama Rao Pappu, Delhi, India, Indian Books Centre, First Edition, 1995.

Fitz, Hope K., "Intuition: Its Nature and Uses," an article published in the *Moksa Journal,* Volume IV, Number 1, November 1987, New York, Bajra Press of Yoga Ananda Ashram, Inc.

Other Works Cited in the Book or Used for Research

A Sourcebook in Indian Philosophy, ed. by Sarvepalli Radhakrishnan and Charles Moore, New Jersey, Princeton University Press, c. 1957, ISBN 0-691-01958-4.

Contemporary Indian Philosophy, ed. by S. Radhakrishnan and J.H. Muirhead, London, George Allen & Unwin Ltd., 1936.

Beat, Steven, and Kellner, Douglas, *Postmodern Theory,* New York, The Guilford Press, c. 1991.

Smith, Huston, *The Religions of Man,* New York, Harper & Row Publishers, c. 1958.

Wendt, Herbert, *In Search of Adam,* tr. from the German by James Cleugh, Boston, Houghton Mifflin Company, c. 1955.

INDEX